10.95

Feminine Sentences

UNIVERSITY OF

Feminine Sentences

Essays on Women and Culture

Janet Wolff

Polity Press

Copyright © Janet Wolff 1990

First published 1990 by Polity Press
in association with Basil Blackwell

Editorial office:
Polity Press, 65 Bridge Street,
Cambridge CB2 1UR, UK

Marketing and production:
Basil Blackwell Ltd
108 Cowley Road, Oxford OX4 1JF, UK

ISBN 0 7456 0751 9
ISBN 0 7456 0855 8 (pbk)

British Library Cataloguing in Publication Data

A CIP catalogue record for this book is available from
the British Library.

Typeset in 10½ on 12pt Sabon
by Colset Private Limited, Singapore
Printed in Great Britain by T.J. Press Ltd, Padstow, Cornwall

7|7|93 50

*For Veronica and Eleanor,
my sisters*

Contents

Acknowledgements

'The Culture of Separate Spheres: The Role of Culture in Nineteenth-Century Public Life' was originally published in Janet Wolff and John Seed (eds.), *The Culture of Capital: Art, Power and the Nineteenth-Century Middle Class* (Manchester, Manchester University Press, 1988).

'The Invisible *Flâneuse*: Women and the Literature of Modernity' was originally published in *Theory, Culture & Society*, 2, 3 (1985).

'Feminism and Modernism' was originally published in Andrew Milner and Chris Worth (eds.), *Discourse and Difference: Post-Structuralism, Feminism and the Moment of History* (Centre for General and Comparative Literature, Monash University, Australia, 1990).

'Women's Knowledge and Women's Art' was originally published as an Occasional Paper by the Institute for Cultural Policy Studies, Griffith University, Brisbane, Australia, 1989.

'Postmodern Theory and Feminist Art Practice' was originally published in Roy Boyne and Ali Rattansi (eds.), *Postmodernism and Society* (London, Macmillan, 1990).

'Texts and Institutions: Problems of Feminist Criticism' was originally published in French in *Recherches Sociologiques*, 19, 2–3 (1988): special issue on *Sociologie de l'Art*.

Some of the essays included in the present volume have been slightly edited and amended, but they are all substantially the same as in their original place of publication.

List of Illustrations

1

Prospects and Problems for a Postmodern Feminism: An Introduction

Three persistent concerns structure the essays in this book. The first is the commitment to the reinstatement of women in the sociology and the literature of modernity; related to this is the project of exploring women's relationship to modern and postmodern culture. The second is the defence of feminist cultural politics, including a politics of the body. And the third is a mission to challenge the continuing separation of sociological from textual analysis in cultural (including feminist) theory and enquiry.

The essays are founded on two major assumptions, nowhere spelled out or defended, but implicit throughout. In the first place, I have taken it as given that culture is central to gender formation. Art, literature, and film do not simply represent given gender identities, or reproduce already existing ideologies of femininity. Rather they participate in the very construction *of* those identities. Second (and consequently), culture is a crucial arena for the contestation of the social arrangements of gender. Cultural politics, then, is not an optional extra – a respectable engagement in one of the more pleasant sectors of political action. It is a vital enterprise, located at the heart of the complex order which (re)produces sexual divisions in society.

Some of the essays in this collection originally appeared as the statutory feminist contribution to a volume of essays on another theme. (Essays 3, 6 and 7 were published in this form). An important part of the rationale of publication of these essays now alongside one another is to offer resistance to what we might call the 'women and . . .' syndrome, whereby sympathetic and dutiful editors ensure that someone is invited to address the question of gender. This is the perennial problem of feminism (and of other oppositional and critical movements), of whether to intervene with the one-off lecture, the individual chapter or essay, the optional course in a traditional degree programme, thus risking dilution, incorporation, and the too-easy appeasement of others' consciences; or whether to work, teach, and publish separately, aiming for the comprehensive feminist text or women's studies programme. Marginalization or ghettoization. I take the rather pragmatic view that both are worth doing (and that each has its problems). In the present case, I have felt that there was a good deal to be gained by extracting each piece from its original context, and facilitating a reading which follows through these issues of gender and culture without interruption. In the next section I will discuss the rationale of the book, before going on to consider some of the main themes and problems dealt with in the essays which follow.

Modernity, Modernism, Postmodernism

I do not propose to add to the voluminous and constantly expanding literature on definition, characterization and periodization which addresses the terms modernity, modernism and postmodernism. In several of the essays in this collection I discuss and analyse some of the ways in which they have been employed, and identify my own usage. (See particularly 'Feminism and Modernism' and 'Postmodern Theory and Feminist Art Practice'.) Here I want to stress the importance of considering the categories in relation to one another. My discussion of postmodernism and feminism, for example, is approached by way of consideration of the earlier promise, and apparent failure, of modernism. Moreover, I attempt in my essay on postmodernism to suggest the continuities between the best postmodern practice and the project of modernism itself. This is one reason why the essays are arranged chronologically, in order of period under discussion, rather than in order of writing or publication. Thus I begin with questions of gender and culture in the mid-nineteenth century, go on in the next essay to discuss women and modernity at the turn of the century, and then, in the following essays, consider women in relation to the history of modernism during this century, and in relation to the postmodern world and culture of the late twentieth century.

More important, the relationship between modern*ity* and moder-n*ism* is too often ignored (or sometimes assumed). As I argue in essays 3 and 4, these are not the same thing. Nor can we take it for granted that modernism in art is the representation of modernity (that is, the experience of the modern world). Raymond Williams has provided a tentative outline for examining the possible connec-tions between these phenomena – between a mode of expression and a social experience – and this is discussed in essay 4.[1] And as I also show in that essay, women's apparent exclusion from modernism has been related by some commentators to their social exclusion from key experiences in the modern world, which have been taken to be central to the modernist canon (city life, the First World War, and so on). Whether or not this is so (and here I have agreed with those who have rejected the narrower definition of 'modernism' which automatically excludes women's work), the point is that *what* women write or paint is clearly related to their experiences. Those experiences, in the nineteenth century, early twentieth century and now, have been very different from those of men. The work of women modernists in art and literature, which is now being rediscovered and re-evaluated, is just as much an expres-sion of and response to the 'modern' experience as the officially acclaimed work of male modernists.

The two essays which follow this introduction are thus concerned with the situation of women in society, first in mid-nineteenth-century England during the development and consolidation of the culture and ideology of 'separate spheres' (though, as I also point out, this process was far from uniform or complete), and secondly in the modern city, from the mid-nineteenth century (when Baudelaire first addressed the question of city life) to the early twentieth century. The confinement of women to the domestic sphere, the problematic nature of their appearance in the public arena, and the consequent irrelevance of most of the literature of modernity (sociological as well as literary) to women's experience need to be spelled out before we can go on to consider contemporary forms of cultural expression and their relationship to social experience. The discussion of women's art in the following essay (essay 4) can then be better understood, in relation to a different conception of what constitutes 'the modern'. It is not, to emphasize this point again, that the art of the modern period is necessarily modernist; this is a matter of formal innovation, as well as of content. But we can begin to see that women innovators (that is, modernists) were also producing important work, whose invisibility in the history of the arts is explained by a male-centred definition of the features of the modern.

Textual, Sexual, Social Critique

The tendency to separate questions of modernity from questions of modernism (or – another version of the same mistake – to assume their identity) is part of the more general limitation of much work in cultural analysis, including feminist analysis. This is the third of my concerns listed at the beginning of this introduction, namely the separation of sociological from textual analysis. This issue is spelled out in detail in the penultimate essay ('Texts and Institutions: Problems of Feminist Criticism'), but the inhibiting dichotomy it attacks underlies many of the obstacles confronted by feminists, which are identified in the other essays. As I have argued, the exclusion of women and their experience from accounts of life in the modern city, discussed in the essay 'The Invisible *Flâneuse*: Women and the Literature of Modernity', is largely the product of an extremely partial sociology of modern life, which perceives and describes the world of men, while ignoring totally the real social and experiential situation of women at the turn of the century. But it is equally true that we cannot *resolve* questions of women's relation to modernism purely at the level of representation. In 'Feminism and Modernism' I consider the paintings of Mary Cassatt and Gwen John, for example, suggesting ways in which these might be read as expressions of women's specific experience of the modern world. An adequate exploration of this issue, however, would need to be based on a social-historical exploration of women's actual participation in the social arrangements, institutions, and processes of city life, matters which are only touched on in the context of that essay.

The fact is that a good deal of feminist cultural analysis is essentially textual analysis. Novels and other texts are reread by feminists as the complex expression of women's lives (or, if they are by men, of men's distortions of those lives). Artistic practices and cultural works by women artists and writers are assessed for their subversive, critical, or mobilizing potential, but this assessment is in purely textual terms. The assumption appears to be that the identification of politically correct features of a work would be enough to guarantee its effectivity (whether the features proposed are celebratory, critical, or deconstructive – see essays 6 and 8 for a discussion of these alternatives). We may certainly point out the potential advantages, limitations, or dangers of such textual politics, but in the end we cannot legislate about effectivity without reference to the specific circumstances of readers and viewers.[2] Annette Kuhn, contrasting the strengths and weaknesses of feminist work on film melodrama and feminist analysis of television soap operas, concludes by urging the combination of the textual analysis characteristic of the former with the sociological study of viewers of the latter.[3] Whatever the potential readings of a text and the implied readers or spectators detected in the work, only a sociology of audiences, readers, and viewers will tell us what a work will *actually* mean at its reception. (And only a social-historical approach to production will enable us to develop an account of the possible or probable meanings of a work in relation to its moment of origin.) Again, in those essays in which I deal with cultural politics (mainly essays 6 and 8), this dimension is so far inadequately examined. A systematic exploration of feminist art practice and of body politics would necessarily involve a serious attempt to relate textual strategies to practices of reading and viewing, and to the contexts and institutions of reception.

A similar argument about the ultimate failure of a feminist aesthetics based solely on textual analysis has been made in a recent book by Rita Felski. With regard to literature, and to feminist literary theory, she demonstrates the misguided nature of any attempts to define a feminist aesthetic or feminist cultural politics in abstract, general, or textual terms, arguing that 'the political value of literary texts from the standpoint of feminism can be determined only by an investigation of their social functions and effects in relation to the interests of women in a particular historical context'.[4] In other words, sexual and textual politics cannot be separated from social analysis. The central topic of the later essays in this collection – cultural politics – should be addressed, just as much as the earlier concerns of women and modernity/modernism, in terms of sociological as well as textual categories.

Questions of Cultural Politics

It is with this caution in mind that we should approach the issue of feminist cultural politics. Varieties of cultural practice have been claimed as appropriate for women's voice and for a feminist intervention in culture, modernism and postmodernism amongst them. As the essays in this book attempt to show, the promise for women of new forms of expression has invariably appeared to be cancelled out by the inevitable exclusion of women from what becomes a predominantly male canon. Thus women are more or less invisible in mainstream histories of modernism. Already the prominent names in postmodern art and literature are mainly those of men. The institutions of cultural production (including the practices of criticism and of academic disciplines) continue their age-old habit of writing women out of the account. Despite this, some feminists have insisted on the availability, and potential, for women of both modernist and postmodern strategies, and I have endorsed particular versions of this claim in the essays that follow.

In essays 6 and 8, I review some of the issues involved in the confrontation between celebratory (humanist) cultural politics and postmodern (deconstructive) strategies, identifying the problems involved in the uncritical presentation of images (albeit positive ones) of women on the one hand and the limitations of an abstruse textual practice on the other. Although I have argued in favour of the destabilizing and critical methods of certain postmodern techniques, my acknowledgement there of the strategic value of celebratory art, which works to create new and positive images of women, should be seen in relation to the insistence on the link between the textual and the social. It is a matter of audience and of potential readings, and not solely a matter of aesthetic orthodoxy. In other words, although it is only those critical and deconstructive practices which can expose the logic of patriarchal systems of representation in order to clear a space for a feminist politics of culture, it may well be that the more direct approach of a celebratory aesthetic engages with particular viewers or readers in specific situations and at specific moments. Such strategies of representation leave untouched the problematic category of 'woman' and avoid the task of analysing its construction (in social relations, ideology, and in representation itself), thereby taking the risk of subscribing to the essentialism of belief in the inherently

'female' or 'feminine'. But they may have their own logic of dislocation, enabling a particular kind of alienation effect which is the
result of substituting new and unfamiliar images for those available
in the dominant culture. As more direct aids to the mobilization of
consciousness, too, clearly this cultural politics is often most
effective. Again, the sociology of reception makes absolutely clear
the illegitimacy of insisting on a 'correct' textual practice for
feminism.

The politics of the body, discussed in the final essay in this
collection, raises very directly many of the issues at stake in the
question of feminist cultural politics. In that essay I consider the
dangers for feminism of engaging in a simple celebration of
the female body – dangers of appropriation, misreading, and essentialism. With particular reference to transformations in dance, from
the classical ballet through modern to postmodern dance, I suggest
that the most effective body politics is one which incorporates its
own acknowledgement of the materiality of the body, and whose
project, amongst other things, is to address and deconstruct the
(idea of the) body in contemporary culture. In this particular area
postmodern practices manifest a greater degree of this self-
reflexivity than modern dance. But, as I say in my essay on postmodernism, it often strikes me that the characteristics of modernism
can sound almost identical to those of postmodernism: self-
reflexivity, irony, juxtaposition, alienation effects, laying bare the
device (making clear the nature of the medium and of representation itself). Inasmuch as the key difference is sometimes said
to consist in postmodernism's rejection of theory, or 'grand
narratives', then this raises problems, not least for feminism.

The Problem of Theory and the Problem of 'Women'

Feminism has an important investment in the critique of theory.
The exposure of theory and philosophy as the limited vision of
white, western, middle-class male thought (discussed in essays 5
and 6) renders it a priority for feminists, and other excluded groups,
to challenge this discourse. This is why post-structuralist theory,
deconstructionism, and postmodernism have been thought to be so
valuable for feminist politics. They enable the destabilization of
patriarchal thought, and the political critique of idelogies of science
and 'objectivity'. But the total abandonment of theory poses

problems for feminism. In general, the commitment to radical relativism is necessarily disingenuous – there can be no 'view from nowhere'.[5] And for feminists, the refusal of a theoretical position or a fundamental model of analysis (such as the structures of gender inequality in society) would obviously undercut our project and our politics.

The desire to deconstruct is not just the product of the critique of androcentric thought. It has also emerged from the important recognition that feminism itself has been a partial, and excluding, discourse, representing the experience of white, middle-class, heterosexual women. Some women have therefore argued that differences among women can only be acknowledged by a feminism which refuses to 'totalize', and which eschews the stable categories of theory in favour of the ceaseless play of signifiers. But here the same problems arise. Susan Bordo argues that such radical deconstructive strategies have the ironic effect of colluding with patriarchy, since a feminist politics requires the positing of, and commitment to, a unified feminist consciousness. As she shows, the search for an adequate account of the diversities among women is an impossible one (since such diversities are potentially infinite). Recognition of the limits of specific theories and analyses does not entail abandoning these, and insistence on the commonalities of women's experience (and oppression) is both valid and crucial for feminist critique.[6]

What this means is that we have to retain a commitment to theory, while recognizing its provisional nature. Other feminists have opted for the more fragmentary methods of a postmodernism which has broken any lingering attachments to the rational project of modernism.[7] Others attempt to find a middle way, retaining the ambivalence of developing theory while, as Sandra Harding puts it, 'embracing the instability of the analytic categories'.[8] While the debate about feminism and postmodernism continues in numerous journals and collections of essays, here I reiterate my own position, spelled out in relation to the visual arts in essay 6 – namely that an entirely dispersed and fragmented politics is both misconceived and impossible, and that any postmodernism of value inherits both the rational project and the critical self-reflexivity of the best of modernist thought.

The question of 'woman' is related to the problem of theory, for post-structuralist theories have exposed the essentialism of humanist thought. This critique applies equally to humanist feminism. The subject (including the female subject) is constructed in discourse and representation and is thus not a stable, unified category. This has led some feminists (often in connection with the debates about theory just reviewed) to reject the category 'woman' and the collectivity 'women', in favour of a textual fluidity in which the subject is constantly deferred. Susan Bordo's comments are equally pertinent here, as are the conclusions drawn by Denise Riley and Mary Poovey. Riley's argument is that though 'women' are historically and discursively constructed, differently at different moments and in different situations, and that 'women' is therefore an unstable category, nevertheless it is a category we must continue to employ. As she says, 'it is compatible to suggest that "women" don't exist – while maintaining a politics of "as if they existed" – since the world behaves as if they unambiguously did.'[9] Mary Poovey makes much the same point, when she argues that we need to work out 'some way to think both women and "women" ', since real historical women *do* exist, despite the theoretical recognition that the subject must be de-centred.[10]

Feminine Sentences

Virginia Woolf believed that modernism offered the opportunity to women of writing their own experience, employing the 'sentence of the feminine gender' (see 'Feminism and Modernism'). In the essays that follow I explore the possibility of feminine writing (or painting), and discuss many of the difficulties contained in such a notion. As Rita Felski has pointed out, there is nothing inherently feminist in experimental (or, for that matter, any other kind of) writing.[11] And, as I have argued here, we cannot assess texts in purely intrinsic terms if we hope to discover their critical or liberatory potential, for this is a matter of situated readings and viewings. Nevertheless it seems reasonable to suppose that new forms of cultural expression, by virtue of the fact that their very existence challenges and dislocates dominant narratives and discourses, provide the space for different voices to speak and for hitherto silenced subjects to articulate their experience. This is why both modernism and postmodernism have offered such an opportunity to women. To demonstrate the ultimate failure of modernism, the incorporation of each into the establishment, the speedy domination of both by men, is not to deny their initial, and even continuing, potential. If we distinguish between modernism as institution and modernism as cultural and political strategy, as Griselda Pollock has suggested we do (see essay 6), we need not conclude that the legitimation of the former entails the neutralization of the latter.

But the title *Feminine Sentences* is not intended just to refer to Virginia Woolf and the debate about modernism. In part, I wanted to signal by it the secondary meaning of the word 'sentence', indicating an exploration of the constraints and restrictions experienced by women in a patriarchal culture. Women, in this sense, are sentenced to containment and silence. More important, this collection is intended as a contribution to the overthrow of that 'sentence', and to the process whereby women find ways to intervene in an excluding culture, and to articulate their own experience. Feminine sentences are those formulations and expressions, in a variety of cultural forms and media, of women's own voice.

NOTES

1   Raymond Williams, 'The Metropolis and the Emergence of Modernism', in Edward Timms and David Kelley (eds), *Unreal City: Urban Experience in Modern European Literature and Art*, (Manchester, Manchester University Press, 1985).
2   See Fred Pfeil, 'Postmodernism and our Discontent', *Socialist Review*, 87/88 (1986).
3   Annette Kuhn, 'Women's genres', *Screen*, 25, 1 (1984).
4   Rita Felski, *Beyond Feminist Aesthetics: Feminist Literature and Social Change* (Cambridge, Mass., Harvard University Press, 1989), p. 2.
5   Thomas Nagel, *The View from Nowhere* (Oxford, Oxford University Press, 1986).
6   Susan Bordo, 'Feminism, Postmodernism and Gender-Scepticism', in Linda Nicholson (ed.), *Feminism/Postmodernism* (New York and London, Routledge, 1990).
7   For example Jane Flax, 'Postmodernism and Gender Relations in Feminist Theory', *Signs*, 12, 4 (Summer 1987). See also Donna Haraway, 'A Manifesto for Cyborgs: Science, Technology, and Socialist Feminism in the 1980s', *Socialist Review*, 80 (1983).
8   Sandra Harding, 'The Instability of the Analytic Categories of Feminist Theory', *Signs*, 11, 4 (Summer 1986).
9   Denise Riley, *'Am I That Name?' Feminism and the Category of*

'*Women*' *in History* (Minneapolis, University of Minnesota Press, 1988).

10   Mary Poovey, 'Feminism and Deconstruction', *Feminist Studies*, 14, 1 (Spring 1988), p. 53.

11   Felski, *Beyond Feminist Aesthetics*, p. 5.

2

The Culture of Separate Spheres: The Role of Culture in Nineteenth-Century Public and Private Life

Writing in 1851, J.W. Hudson describes the 'liberal and comprehensive scheme of female education' introduced at the Manchester Mechanics' Institute in 1841: 'For less than thirty shillings per quarter, a young lady may receive the elements of what is termed an English education, and be taught the accomplishments now considered necessary to her position, including the French language, drawing, vocal and instrumental music, dancing, modelling, with the useful arts of millinery and dress-making.'[1] The intention of the directors of the Institute was explicitly that of teaching women 'what would make them better wives, sisters, mothers' as well as better 'members of society'.[2] It would be inappropriate and misleading to consider this a simple case of sex discrimination, for we also find that in the girls' school opened there in 1835 the subjects taught were more or less the same as those taught at the boys' school, namely reading, writing, arithmetic, geography, history, and grammar. The boys also learned algebra and geometry, and the girls sewing and knitting.[3] The access of girls and women to culture and to knowledge in the first half of the nineteenth century in England was complex and often con-tradictory. Nevertheless my main argument in this essay will be that the continuing process of the 'separation of spheres' of male and female, public and private, was on the whole reinforced and maintained by cultural ideologies, practices, and institutions. This applies both to women's place in *cultural production* (as artists, authors, patrons, and members of cultural institutions) and to the dominant modes of *cultural representation*, particularly in literature and the visual arts, and their construction of notions of gender. Interwoven with both of these is that nineteenth-century morality that determined which books or paintings would be publicly available (I shall consider a few examples of such extra-aesthetic influence later on), and which spheres of activity were appropriate for men and women. But although my starting point is the separation of spheres, it is important to stress that any implication of a simple determinism must be rejected. The particular focus of this essay on the role of culture does not presuppose either a ready-formed or static 'middle class', or a straightforward economic and ideological 'separation of spheres'. Indeed this separation was constantly and multiply produced (and counteracted) in a variety of sites, including culture and the arts. So, for example, women's exclusion from various areas of productive work did not *entail* their exclusion from painting; rather, the latter was the product of the specific ideologies and practices *of* art and of 'the artist'.[4] My argument that cultural institutions and ideologies contributed to the separation of spheres should not, therefore, be read as either an idealist account (culture as producing social divisions) or a reductionist one (culture as epiphenomenal, merely reflecting existing divisions).

The Separation of Public and Private Life

Leonore Davidoff and Catherine Hall have documented the 'separation of spheres' into the public world of work and politics and the private world of the home, as well as the concomitant development of the domestic ideology that relegated middle-class women to the private sphere.[5] The material separation of work and home, which was the result of both the Industrial Revolution and the growth of suburbs, was clearly the precondition of the general process, though, as Catherine Hall has pointed out, for many families and many occupations this separation did not always occur (for example, in the case of doctors' practices).[6] Working-class women, of course, continued to work. The cult of domesticity was strong among the middle class by the 1830s, emphasizing the sanctity and purity of family life, and the moral task of women as mothers and wives. Women who did continue to work outside the home were increasingly restricted to particular kinds of occupation – servicing rather than productive, and 'women's trades' of teaching, dressmaking, and retail – and excluded from the new financial institutions associated with business.[7] At the same time the 'public world' expanded, providing for men a multitude of additional activities and institutions – banks, political organizations, voluntary societies, and cultural institutions. Women's involvement in these organizations, where it existed at all, was indirect or informal – for example, as visitors, but not officers, of philanthropic societies.[8]

Physically, the separation of spheres was marked, as well as constructed, by both geography and architecture. From the 1830s the more prosperous members of the middle class in the major manufacturing cities began to move out of the town centre, and to build houses in the suburbs. The development of Victoria Park, Manchester, illustrates this move well.

During the early and middle 1830s, the out-of-town villa residence was just beginning to become fashionable. There remain, even today, many examples of this type of property that were put up between about 1835 and 1850. The broad band of country from Greenheys, Chorlton-on-Medlock, the northern parts of Rusholme (i.e. Victoria Park), Plymouth Grove and parts of Longsight and Ardwick contain examples of late Georgian terraces and villa residences. These houses were all occupied by the emerging mercantile class of the city.[9]

Thirty-five such large houses were constructed in Victoria Park between 1837 and 1845.[10] Maurice Spiers describes James Kershaw, one of the earliest residents of Victoria Park (he lived there from 1838 to 1859) as typical of those setting up their homes there. He was a partner in the calico-painting firm of Leese, Callender and Co., having started life as a warehouse lad. He was a member of the Council of the League, an Alderman from 1838 to 1850, Mayor in 1842–3, and MP for Stockport from 1847 to 1859. Interestingly, Spiers also notes that before moving out of the centre of Manchester, Kershaw had lived in Great Ancoats Street, where his wife carried on a business as a linen draper.[11] He does not record whether she was able to continue her occupation after the move to the suburbs, but she certainly did not do so from the new address, and it is most unlikely that she travelled into town. Although the extent of suburbanization should not be overestimated (many middle-class families remained in the more central urban areas), where it did occur, the move to the suburbs entailed a clear separation of home and work, and a firm basis for the domestic ideology of the home as haven, and of women as identified with this private sphere. Davidoff and Hall trace the similar development of Birmingham in this period, in the growth of the suburb of Edgbaston.[12]

The design of the new houses themselves usually accorded well with the ideology of separate spheres. With regard to the middle-class elite, Mark Girouard argues that agreement by 1850 about what a 'gentleman's house' should be like included the requirements that 'it should provide decent quarters for servants. It should protect the womanliness of women and encourage the manliness of men.'[13] As well as an extremely complex and often impractical arrangement of rooms, so that children, servants, mothers, and fathers should only coincide at approved times and in approved places,[14] Victorian houses also contained 'an increasingly large and sacrosanct male domain', whose nucleus was the billiard room. The domain often expanded to include the smoking room and the gun room, and sometimes adjoining dressing room and study.[15] Girouard is writing about Victorian country houses. The suburban dwellings of other sections of the middle class were not, of course, built on the same scale; but the same physical separation of domains was apparent, with the increase in the number of servants, and the concern to keep them separate from the family, with the nineteenth-century emphasis on the distinctness of childhood, and with the underlying ideology of the appropriate sensibilities and areas of operation of men and women.[16]

The effects of the clear distinction of 'public' and 'private' spheres, and in particular the limitation of women's existence to the latter, went beyond the lives of the middle classes who first produced it. As Girouard shows, members of the gentry redesigned their houses in accordance with the new social arrangements.[17] More generally, the Victorian domestic ideology, which Catherine Hall has analysed in relation to Evangelical Christianity, extended both 'upward', to the older ruling classes, and 'downward', to the lower-middle and working classes.[18] Although women did continue to work – in factories, in some trades, in certain family businesses – the increasingly dominant ethic of woman's domestic, and subservient, role ignored this fact. Ruskin's well-known catalogue of the disasters wrought throughout the history of literature by the fallibility and corruptibility of men, redeemed only by the purity and wisdom of women, asserts women's 'guiding function' (which, he insists, is quite reconcilable with a 'true wifely subjection').[19] All this is explained by the different male and female characters. The man is 'active, progressive, defensive'; he is

> eminently the doer, the creator, the discoverer, the defender. His intellect is for speculation and invention; his energy for adventure, for war, and for conquest . . . But the woman's power is for rule, not for battle, – and her intellect is not for invention or creation, but for sweet ordering, arrangement, and decision. She sees the qualities of things, their claims, and their places. Her great function is Praise: she enters into no contest, but infallibly adjudges the crown of contest. By her office, and place, she is protected from all danger and temptation. The man, in his rough work in the open world, must encounter all peril and trial: – to him, therefore, must be the failure, the offence, the inevitable error: often he must be wounded, or subdued; often misled; and *always* hardened. But he guards the woman from all this; within his house, as ruled by her, unless she herself has sought it, need enter no danger, no temptation, no cause of error or offence. This is the true nature of home – it is the place of Peace.[20]

There were certainly alternative opinions expressed in the mid-nineteenth century about 'women's proper place' and their appropriate education – for instance, by John Stuart Mill. But the strength of the Ruskinian ideal was enormous, and it was an ideal also upheld by other influential writers of the period, like Thomas Carlyle. Geraldine Jewsbury, author and a friend of the Carlyles, was outraged by his opinion that 'a woman's natural object in the world is to *go out* and find herself some sort of *man her superior* – and obey him loyally and lovingly and make herself as much as possible into *a beautiful reflex* of him!'[21] The persistence of this domestic ideal, in Ruskin's own formulation, is still evident much later in the century. Katherine Chorley, daughter of Edward Hopkins, the managing director of the engineering firm, Mather and Platt, describes her early years in Alderley Edge, just outside Manchester, in the last decades of the century. (By then those moving into the suburbs had to go rather farther afield than Victoria Park.) She writes, somewhat ruefully, about the influences of Ruskin on her own upbringing. Her father, from a Manchester Nonconformist background, had the complete Ruskin 'bound in blue calf', and Katherine Chorley believes 'he must have dipped a good bit' into these texts: 'his ideal of womanhood – a little unfortunately for me as I grew older – was obviously founded on *Sesame and Lilies*'.[22] Her mother, an Ulster Irishwoman, though from a quite different background, shared his views on the education of young women. Chorley writes of her parents:

> They very much disliked any sort of day school which approximated to the high school type. In their opinion, education at an establishment of this kind involved a 'roughening' process, a physical and intellectual scramble combined with contacts whose suitability they would not be able to control. In short, they affirmed the ideals for young women set out in Ruskin's *Sesame and Lilies* and felt that these were not likely to be nourished in a high school.[23]

Domestic life certainly reinforced these ideals:

> Mother was very particular about anything which symbolized decorous behaviour as between males and females. The downstairs lavatory, for instance, was sacrosanct to the men of the family and their guests, the upstairs was reserved with equal exclusiveness to the females. Woe betide me if I was ever found slinking into the downstairs to save time. Conversely, the good breeding and social knowledge of any male guest who was suspected of having used the upstairs while dressing for dinner was immediately called in question.[24]

Relations between husband and wife also conformed to the Ruskinian ideal. 'Throughout their married life (mother) had laid upon herself the plain first duty as she conceived it of carrying father through his troubles and difficulties.' Nevertheless, 'Father might be outwardly masterful, but mother was inwardly the mistress of her own being.'[25]

Domestic Ideology and the Role of Culture

The fact that Geraldine Jewsbury objected to Carlyle's views about women reminds us that Victorian domestic ideology was by no means a monolithic or all-pervasive one. The separation of public and private spheres was not always clearly marked. Many women did work outside the home. And many people, of both sexes, subscribed to some sort of equality of men and women, in education and more generally. For example Tylecote points out that the propagandists of the Mechanics' Institutes had stressed the importance of female education.[26] Nevertheless, the kind of feminine ideal described by Carlyle and Ruskin was powerful and widespread by the mid-nineteenth century. The practices and the institutions of culture and the arts played a considerable part in this, and numerous cases testify to the role of culture in supporting the ideology of separate spheres.

Ruskin's views on society and morality were inseparable from his art criticism. He objected to the nudes of William Mulready (1786–1863) as 'more degraded and bestial than the worst grotesques of the Byzantine or even Indian image makers', and as 'most vulgar, and in the solemn sense of the word, most abominable'.[27] Moreover, although he was an artist himself, he never attended a life-class.[28] Ruskin's influence as an art critic was enormous (although Jeremy Maas certainly overstates the case when he claims of Ruskin that 'he had only to wonder why no-one ever painted apple-trees in blossom for the Academy walls a year later to be covered with orchards full of apple-trees in blossom').[29] Aesthetic judgements were, of course, not always or even primarily posed in moral terms. But in 1855, despite finding Leighton's painting, Cimabue's Celebrated Madonna, 'a very important and very beautiful picture' (an opinion shared by many other reviewers and artists), Ruskin thought Millais's The Rescue, shown at the same Royal Academy exhibition in 1855, a greater picture. Leighton thought that this judgement was based on the belief that 'the joy of a mother over her rescued children is a higher order of emotion than any expressed in my picture'.[30] Whether this tells us the actual basis of Ruskin's judgement, or more about his known views and reputation, the point is the same.

In literature the moral guardians had equally tight control over cultural production – perhaps a greater power in so far as they were often in a position to determine which books were published. In particular, Mudie's circulating library and W.H. Smith's bookstands, central to the success of both authors and publishers, operated on a severe moral code. As J.A. Sutherland writes, 'The two greatest entrepreneurs of fiction in mid-Victorian England, Mudie and W.H. Smith, set themselves to impose middle-class decencies on the English novel.'[31] Mudie's influence, he goes on, was 'frequently a trespass on artistic freedom'. For fear of offending him, Trollope's Barchester Towers, whose success depended on a substantial sale to the circulating library, was censored by the publisher's adviser, who wanted it purged of its 'vulgarity' and 'exaggeration'; an example given by Sutherland of the changes required was the alteration of the phrase 'fat stomach' to 'deep chest'.[32] With somewhat less influence, and coming, in any case, after the event, reviewers of Geraldine Jewsbury's rather turgid romantic novel, Zöe (1845), expressed their shock at a heroine in love with two men (as well as at a critical attitude to religion). Her publisher, Mr Chapman of Chapman and Hall, receiving a letter of complaint from one of Geraldine Jewsbury's own friends, Mrs S. C. Hall, began to worry about the effect the publication would have on him, until reassured by Jane Carlyle.[33] But Jane Carlyle herself, who had obtained the reading of the manuscript by Chapman in the first place, had already persuaded the author, as her biographer puts it, 'into the application of "spotted muslin" to some of the more flagrantly indecorous parts'.[34] Whether because of publishers' fears of disapproval from Mudie's, from Smith's, or from other major buyers, or because of their judgement of readers' moral sensibilities, the assessment of manuscripts was clearly very much in terms of acceptable religious and moral values. The reaction to Mrs Gaskell's Ruth, a novel about the seduction, 'fall', and redemption of an innocent young girl, published in 1853, was even more violent, and upset its author enough to make her ill for some days, and to cause her to think 'I must be an improper woman, without knowing it. I do so manage to shock people'.[35] As far as sexuality was concerned, these debates and editorial checks illustrate not so much a straightforward form of censorship, but rather a careful negotiation of the area, and the formulation in very specific ways of the particular, appropriate, visibility of sexuality at that time.

The direct influence of patrons on the work of painters was surprisingly common in a century when the ideology of the autonomous creative artist was developing. Although the relationship was not one in which, as in the early Renaissance and before, the patron might list the detail of content and use of colour pigment to appear in a commissioned work, it was not unusual for the prospective buyer to specify what he wanted in the work. Henry McConnel, of the Manchester cotton-spinning firm, McConnel and Kennedy, commissioned Turner to paint Keelmen Heaving in Coals by Night. Darcy suggests that McConnel 'most likely wished the artist to contrast the timeless calm of Venice with the industrial bustle of the River Tyne', since he already owned a painting of

Venice.[36] Thomas Plint, a Leeds stockbroker, asked Mulready to paint him a work on a theme from *The Vicar of Wakefield* or from Sir Walter Scott's writings; both were popular sources of paintings in the mid-nineteenth century, and indeed Mulready had already illustrated Scott's novels and the Goldsmith novel, and exhibited and sold paintings on themes from them.[37] It appears that Mulready did not accept this commission, nor one from Prince Albert to paint a copy of one of his *Vicar of Wakefield* paintings, *Choosing the Wedding Gown* (1845).[38] Other artists complied with their patrons' requests, and to that extent the interests and values of buyers came to be represented in some works, although the general effect of this on Victorian paintings cannot be easily summarized. According to Maas, the nude in painting only survived the prudery of the Victorian era because of the more liberal attitudes of the 'new' patrons – the merchants and industrialists of the North and the Midlands, who, he argued, were 'uninhibited by the pruderies of the capital'.[39] But since to a large extent these 'pruderies' were the product of the new middle class itself, another explanation for the persistence and acceptance (sometimes limited, as I have already suggested) of the nude in painting must be found. This is something I shall return to later. Contrary to Maas's view, the evidence seems to suggest the more puritanical influence of the new patrons. (However, as I shall argue later, it is entirely misleading to assume a unitary meaning for a picture, and to ignore, for example, the effects of different contexts or locations of display and the possibility of different *readings* of a work.)

On the rather different issue of religious evangelism (not necessarily coincident with moral prudery) another recorded instance of Thomas Plint's interest in painting documents his success in getting Ford Madox Brown to change his famous painting, *Work* (Plate 1). Having seen the sketches for this painting in 1856, he agreed to buy it, but asked for two changes. On the right of the work, the two standing figures represented are Thomas Carlyle and F.D. Maurice. Plint had requested representations of Carlyle and Charles Kingsley. In his other request, he appears to have been entirely successful in his intercession with the artist. On the left of the painting are depicted four well-dressed women, walking past the labouring men. Brown has responded to Plint's request in a letter written after seeing the preliminary sketches, in which he wrote 'Could you change one of the four *fashionable* young ladies into a *quiet*, *earnest*, *holy*-looking one, with a book or two and *tracts*'? I want *this* put in, for I am much interested in *this* work myself, and know those who are.'[40]

Most paintings were not conceived or modified by their patrons. Many works were painted without a commission, for exhibition and later sale. Many buyers were not Nonconformists or Evangelical Christians, and, among those who were, this was not necessarily reflected in a strict application of their moral and religious code to the arts. So I am not suggesting that the production of culture in nineteenth-century England was dominated and overseen by an elite group of rich and powerful middle-class reformers, who ensured that painting and literature reinforced domestic ideology, bourgeois morality, and the notion of the protected place of women in society. But it is worth identifying the influence of that ideology where it clearly did operate in the production and distribution of culture. To a considerable extent, patrons, critics, reviewers, publishers, and others colluded in the dissemination of a culture which was sanitized and shaped in accordance with the middle-class ideology of separate spheres.) A final example of this, more explicit than most, though from a slightly later period, is discussed in Frances Borzello's article on the origins of the Whitechapel Art Gallery in the East End of London.[41] The Gallery, which was opened in 1901, had begun with a series of annual fine art exhibitions organized for the poor of the area from 1881 to 1898. The paintings shown at these exhibitions were an impressive selection, even though the premises (a school) were temporary and unsatisfactory. The first exhibition, in 1881, included works by Watts, Leighton, and Burne-Jones, and paintings first exhibited at the Royal Academy were often lent to the Whitechapel exhibitions. Artists and lenders were extremely generous in their support of these exhibitions. Queen Victoria herself lent three paintings in 1887 and two in 1889.[42] Audiences were large: 10,000 visited the exhibition in 1881, 47,000 in 1885, 55,000 in 1890, and 76,000 in 1892. Sales of catalogues were also high: 4,600 in 1882 and 16,000 in 1885 for example.[43] Although, as Borzello says, we do not really know what audiences thought of the works shown, apart from the interpretation of their success by the organizers of the exhibition, the availability of two or three hundred paintings in the East End each year was remarkable, and the clear popularity of certain works, shown by an annual vote for the favourite painting, tells us something about popular taste. (It seems that 'pathetic' subjects were popular, but landscapes were not.) Most important, however, was the motivation of the principal organizers, and the mediation of their views through captions to the paintings, catalogue entries and commentaries, and gallery talks. The exhibitions were the inspiration and production of the Reverend Samuel A. Barnett, Vicar of St Jude's, Whitechapel, and his wife, Henrietta Barnett, social reformers who had faith in the role of art in 'de-brutalising' the poor, and educating them into Christian values. Hence Borzello quotes the caption to a replica of Raphael's *Madonna del Cardellino*, exhibited in 1886, which read: 'In this woman there are the nobleness, and the self-forgetting, ever-watchful care of a true mother. In the children there are the friendship and the tenderness which are ever found in a true home.' A catalogue entry in the same year linked the Holy Family implicitly with the families of Whitechapel. 'The great masters painted the Virgin and Child in likeness of the people they knew; in their eyes every home had the possibility of the highest.'[44] Even the popularity vote each year may well, Borzello suggests, have been affected by the hanging policy of the organizers, which gave prominence to particularly uplifting works.

Women and the Institutions of Culture

So far, I have considered the role of culture in producing and maintaining the social divisions of gender. But culture does not simply reflect social life, responding to transformations in ideology by producing different images and texts. Nineteenth-century cultural practices and institutions were also changed by those same processes which produced the middle class and its ethic. With regard to gender divisions, there were two related important processes: the increasing privatization of leisure, and the virtual exclusion of women from 'public' cultural institutions of various types. In these ways, too, nineteenth-century culture reinforced the separation of spheres.

The increasing class segregation of leisure which began in the late eighteenth century was accompanied by a trend to private leisure – either centred on the home (reading, playing music, gardening) or based on the family (holidays, for example).[45] Those entertainments or cultural activities which did take place in the more public arena, like sports, were almost exclusively male. Women's leisure was confined to the home, particularly among the middle class. As Cunningham says, 'the general rule was that any woman in a public place of leisure, and unaccompanied by husband or other suitable male, was a prostitute.'[46] Women were not able to frequent pubs, coffee houses, or eating places other than pastry-cooks' and confectioners' shops.[47] When accompanied by men, however, women might attend the theatre, particularly in the second half of the century when theatres, having excluded the working class by a variety of measures, including the price of tickets, became 'respectable'.[48] With the rise of musical and concert life in many large cities, too, another respectable public arena for mixed audiences opened up, although a good deal of musical activity and performance occurred in the more private location of people's homes. In mid-century Leeds, for example.

There was no sharp dividing line between the worlds of family, amateur and professional music. The Leeds Musical Soirées, started in 1848, were organized by a select society which included Heatons, Marshalls, Kitsons and Heys among its members. They met in members' houses and occupied the intervals between selections from Handel. Mendelssohn and Wesley with refreshments, including sherry and port.[49]

But many of the major new cultural institutions of the nineteenth century were men's institutions: the literary and philosophical societies, the various scientific societies,[50] statistical societies, gentlemen's clubs and societies. In Birmingham, women were

virtually excluded . . . from many of the meetings of the new clubs and societies, social and scientific as well as political, which were springing up in this period. Examples would be the earliest known Birmingham Book Club probably established around 1750, the Brotherly Society (1776), the Philosophical Institution (1800), the Mechanics' Institute (1825), the Chamber of Manufacturers which grew out of the Commercial Committee of the late 1770s. A similar pattern was followed by the numerous philanthropic societies organized around the provision of medical care and education for the poor.[51]

Women were generally not allowed places as members of committees, or as book borrowers; they might, as in the case of the Birmingham Athenaeum (1839), be able to attend public lectures, but not the weekly meetings or classes; nor were they permitted to go into the reading rooms.[52] Ashton's centenary history of the Manchester Statistical Society (founded in 1833), appends a list of all the Reports and Papers produced by the Society. In the first fifty years of its existence, only two papers out of over three hundred were written by women, both in 1868–9, and one of these was a criticism of another paper.[53] In Kargon's account of science in Victorian Manchester, the only references to women's involvement are to gifts received by institutions from a Miss Brackenbury and from Lady Whitworth as one of the Whitworth legatees.[54]

Indeed, women's traditional role as patron and supporter of intellectual and cultural development continued in the Victorian era. Rich women could give donations to scientific and philan-thropic enterprises, or help in the setting up and running of cultural activities. But women's access to cultural production continued to be extremely limited. Only in 1860 was the first female admitted to the Royal Academy Schools.[55] In other schools of art, provision was made for girls and women – for example, at the Glasgow School of Design, opened in 1844.[56] Where art education was mainly intended for male artisans, female pupils were more likely to be middle-class, and the reasons given for the provision of this educa-tion were usually in terms of helping them to acquire 'an honourable occupation'.[57] On the whole, the art education of ladies remained the province of the private drawing masters, and here the chief purpose was 'to occupy maidens' minds with a harmless pursuit'.[58] The majority of Mulready's private pupils were women, and their education was much in line with this ideology. Mulready himself, however, encouraged his female pupils and took their work very seriously, perhaps, as Heleniak suggests, as a result of his early marriage to an artist, Elizabeth Varley.[59]

From the information available about women painters in Manchester in the first half of the nineteenth century, it appears that although many women did paint, they did not set themselves up as artists. Those who did paint, and even exhibit work, tended to restrict their subject-matter to themes of still life and flowers. This confirms the general trend identified by Parker and Pollock as the marginalization of women artists into certain kinds of paintings, which were accordingly downgraded in status, flower painting being a particularly common genre for women artists.[60] There were exceptions – women who attempted classical or historical sub-jects, despite the severe limitation of access imposed by, amongst other things, exclusion from the life-class.[61] But the majority of women painters limited themselves to 'women's subjects' and exhibited as amateurs, or as teachers and governesses, rather than as artists.

The separation of public and private spheres also operated to the disadvantage of women writers, although the novel was much less problematically a woman's occupation. Exclusion from public life limited the area of experience from which female authors might write, as well as placing practical constraints on their lives as authors. When Mrs Gaskell wanted to visit London in 1849 to see her publisher and to meet people in the literary world, she had to find another woman to travel with her as chaperone, since her husband could not leave his work in Manchester, and 'it was unthinkable for a married lady to go up to London alone'.[62] Geraldine Jewsbury, another Manchester writer, who was a contemporary and neighbour of the Gaskells, and unmarried, appears to have moved with more freedom; but she, as her biographer records, was a more spirited and 'masculine' woman, who smoked cigarettes and proposed to men.[63] Ellen Moers has summed up the situation of the nineteenth-century woman writer:

> Male writers have always been able to study their craft in university or coffee-house, group themselves into movements or coteries, search out predecessors for guidance or patronage, collaborate or fight with their contemporaries. But women through most of the nineteenth century were barred from the universities, isolated in their own homes, chaperoned in travel, painfully restricted in friendship. The personal give-and-take of the literary life was closed to them.[64]

Cultural Representation and the Separation of Spheres

The institutions of culture in the nineteenth century confirmed and reinforced the separation of male and female worlds and the ideology of femininity and domesticity. At the same time, the forms of cultural representation reproduced that ideology, though often, as Tony Davies and others have pointed out, in ambiguous (and sometimes subversive) ways.[65] Patricia Stubbs argues that the novel, by its very nature, enshrines women in the 'private':

> The novel . . . is inherently bound up with the notion of a private life, which has its own autonomous moral standards and values . . . This is peculiarly damaging to women. For within bourgeois society women

are confined to this private, largely domestic world, and have become the focus of a powerful ideology which celebrates private experience and relationships as potent sources of human satisfaction . . . Richardson's *Pamela* then, initiated what has always been a fundamental association in the novel between women and private life. It is from this association that all the familiar images of women in fiction are derived – the virgin heroine, the wife and mother, the prostitute, the spinster, the mistress, the redundant middle-aged woman, the single mother. Though we may deplore this narrow range of 'types' of women represented in fiction, it is important to recognize that they are rooted in the very origins of the form and that they are part of a very strong tradition.[66]

In painting too it is not difficult to make the association between domestic ideology and its representation in art. The public world is inhabited by men; woman's place is in the home. The limits of women's social role are emphasized by dire warnings of the wages of sin. The 'fallen woman' painted by Egg, Hunt, and Redgrave was a 'Victorian preoccupation', treated also (though without enthusiasm) by Mulready,[67] and particularly popular in Victorian theatre, where the 'woman with a past' also appears with great frequency.[68] Egg's painting of *Past and Present* (Plate 2) (a set of three shown at the Royal Academy in 1858, considering the fate of the unfaithful wife, who ends her days as a homeless prostitute sheltering under Waterloo Bridge) drew 'crowds of sensation-seekers eager to be outraged', as well as (or perhaps because of) the shocked reaction of the *Athenaeum*: 'There must be a line drawn as to where the horrors that should not be painted for public and innocent sight begin, and we think Mr Egg has put one foot at least beyond this line.'[69]

This is not the place to attempt an archaeology or psychoanalysis of meanings in representation. However, it is important to stress the problematic nature of the apparent association of domestic ideology with cultural forms or images. In Raymond Williams's view, the 'bourgeois fiction' of the 1840s is also the locus of alternative cultural values of subordinate classes and of elements repressed by the dominant bourgeois ideology; it is only in the second-rate fiction of family-magazine serials and religious or temperance tracts that the 'explicit, conscious bourgeois values' appeared in their purity.[70] The fascination of the 'fallen woman', then, is not only explained in terms of the reassurances afforded to those who conform to the domestic and sexual ideology of the period. Even in the dominant culture, the alternative is expressed in a variety of ways. I conclude this essay by very briefly suggesting how this operated in the case of sexuality – a central theme of domestic ideology.

In the first place, as the *Athenaeum* review itself hints, a more private showing might be considered appropriate. The paintings hung in billiard rooms or in gentlemen's clubs were more risqué than those hung in family rooms and public exhibitions. Mulready produced private drawings of couples embracing, dressed and undressed. As his biographer points out, 'the restrictions which governed his exhibited courtship scenes contrast with the sensual abandonment expressed in the poses of his private lovers – not, by the way, an unusual dichotomy in the work of artists.'[71]

Second, the art and literature of explicit sexuality is transferred more radically to the secret and illicit underworld of pornography, documented in the case of Victorian literature by Steven Marcus,[72] just as the actual sexuality of young middle-class men found an outlet through meetings and casual liaisons at music halls and fairs, barred to 'respectable' women.[73] Third, sexuality appears legitimately, though displaced, through the device of representing the exotic. For example, in high Victorian painting the nude which would have shocked in contemporary scenes is somehow acceptable when set in Ancient Greece or Rome. As Jeremy Maas says, 'the neo-classical painters were able to paint nudes freely by placing them in varying degrees of deshabille in the *tepidarium, frigidarium* or *apodyterium*.'[74] The work of Alma-Tadema, Lord Leighton, Poynter, Edwin Long, and Albert Moore provides the major examples of this neo-classical painting, which was enormously successful. Long's *Babylonian Marriage Market* (1875) was commissioned for 1,700 guineas by Edward Hermon of Henley-on-Thames, and it was sold at Christie's in 1882 for £6,615, a sale-room record until 1892. The work depicts a number of lightly-clad young women, being sold off in order of beauty to potential husbands. Taking it as an exotic subject. Ruskin was able to find it 'of great merit', commenting that it was worthy of purchase by the Anthropological Society. The critical notices in all the journals, including the *Athenaeum*, which had objected so strongly to Egg's moral tale, were highly favourable.[75]

Fourth, repressed sexuality appears in the spaces and ambiguities of the text or work itself. There is already a large literature on the possibility of feminist readings of classic texts of nineteenth-century fiction.[76] In painting as in literature, there is invariably a multiplicity of meanings in a text, and it is possible to expose the contradictions of the work in relation to the contradictory and contested area of sexuality and gender in social life. Caroline Arscott's analysis of William Holman Hunt's *The Awakening Conscience* employs semiotic and psychoanalytic methods to analyse the possible contemporary interpretations of this particular 'fallen woman' image, stressing the *pleasure* in looking (for male viewers) as well as the moral warning, and suggesting that particular features of content and form offered a reading of the text which perhaps did not conform to the usual formula of seduction–guilt–punishment–death.[77] And more generally, it is clear that such representations operate to bring sexuality into discourse, as Foucault has shown to have been the case across a range of disciplines and discourses in the nineteenth century.[78] The implications of this for female viewers would therefore be worth exploring, in the way that contemporary film criticism has been occupied with the investigation of the nature of the female gaze in relation to patriarchal representations on the screen.[79]

This essay has been primarily concerned with the role of culture in producing, confirming, and maintaining (and, perhaps, subverting) ideologies of gender and sexuality. I hope to have made it clear that culture is not a passive vehicle for the transmission of already existing social values and ideologies, but rather that representation participates actively in the *construction* of such values. Thus the very notions of sexuality, femininity, masculinity, and so on were in process of construction – in art and literature as much as in moral or political discourse. As Lynda Nead has argued, 'rather than viewing pictures as illustrations or reflections of Victorian morality, these representations have to be seen as the site of production of discourses on morality and sexuality'.[80] I have argued that the institutions and discourses of culture in the nineteenth century operated in such a way as to aid in the construction and maintenance of the ideology of the separation of public and private spheres, and of women's domestic role. Although by no means uniform or complete, this separation was to set the terms of existence for men and women of all classes into the twentieth century. At the same time, the contradictions and constraints of these social divisions and their moral regulation were manifest in those very texts which ostensibly reinforced them.

NOTES

Thanks to James Donald, Caroline Arscott, and Griselda Pollock for comments on this essay at an earlier stage.

1   J. W. Hudson, *The History of Adult Education* (The Woburn Press, 1969), p. 135.

2   Mabel Tylecote, *The Mechanics' Institutes of Lancashire and Yorkshire before 1851*, (Manchester, Manchester University Press, 1957), p. 186. The quotation is from a speech made in 1846 by Daniel Stone, managing director of the Institute, and printed in the 1847 Annual Report.

3   Ibid., p. 184.

4   See Griselda Pollock's article, 'Vision, Voice and Power: Feminist Art History and Marxism', *Block*, 6 (1982).

5   Leonore Davidoff *et al.*, 'Landscape with Figures: Home and Community in English Society', in Juliet Mitchell and Ann Oakley (eds), *The Rights and Wrongs of Women* (Harmondsworth, Penguin, 1976); Catherine Hall, 'The Early Formation of Victorian Domestic Ideology', in Sandra Burman (ed.), *Fit Work for Women* (London, Croom Helm, 1979); Catherine Hall, 'The Butcher, the Baker, the Candlestickmaker: The Shop and the Family in the Industrial Revolution', in Elizabeth Whitelegg *et al.* (eds), *The Changing Experience of Women* (Oxford, Martin Robertson, 1982); Catherine Hall, 'Gender Divisions and Class Formation in the Birmingham Middle Class, 1780–1850', in Raphael Samuel (ed.), *People's History and Socialist Theory* (London, Routledge & Kegan Paul, 1981). The public/private division has also been developed in feminist history in the United States during the 1970s.

6   In Raphael Samuel (ed.), *People's History and Socialist Theory*, p. 169. In *Family Fortunes: Men and Women of the English Middle Class, 1780–1850* (London, Hutchinson, 1987), published after this essay was written, Davidoff and Hall show that the supposed 'separation of spheres' was an extremely complex (and in many ways *limited*) affair.

7   Ibid., pp. 168–9.

8   Ibid., p. 171.

9   Maurice Spiers, *Victoria Park Manchester: A Nineteenth-Century Suburb in its Social and Administrative Context* (Manchester, Manchester University Press, 1976), p. 2.

10   Ibid., p. 12.

11   Ibid., p. 6.

12   Leonore Davidoff and Catherine Hall, 'The Architecture of Public and Private Life: English Middle-Class Society in a Provincial Town 1780–1850', in D. Fraser and A. Sutcliffe (eds), *The Pursuit of Urban History* (London, Edward Arnold, 1983).

13   Mark Girouard, *The Victorian Country House* (New Haven, Conn., Yale University Press, 1979), p. 16.
14   Ibid., p. 28.
15   Ibid., pp. 34–6.
16   See Davidoff and Hall, 'Architecture of Public and Private Life'.
17   Girouard *Victorian Country House* pp. 5–8.
18   In Sandra Burman (ed.), *Fit Work for Women* and in Whitelegg *et al.* (eds), *Changing Experience of Women*.
19   John Ruskin, 'Of Queen's Gardens', in *Sesame and Lilies* (London, George Allen & Sons, 1913), p. 135.
20   Ibid., pp. 135–7. (Italics in original.)
21   Susanne Howe, *Geraldine Jewsbury, her Life and Errors* (London, George Allen & Unwin, 1935), p. 105 (Italics in original.)
22   Katherine Chorley, *Manchester Made Them* (London, Faber & Faber, 1950), pp. 178–9. (It is worth noting, however, that Katherine Chorley wrote her account in her sixties, publishing the book in the mid-twentieth century, so that her regret at the strictness of her upbringing may well be coloured in retrospect by the more liberal views of this century.)
23   Ibid., pp. 186–7.
24   Ibid., pp. 101–2.
25   Ibid., pp. 110, 111.
26   Mabel Tylecote, *Mechanics' Institutes of Lancashire and Yorkshire*, p. 263.
27   Kathryn Moore Heleniak, *William Mulready* (New Haven, Conn., Yale University Press, 1980), p. 158.
28   Jeremy Maas, *Victorian Painters* (Barrie & Rockliff, The Cresset Press, 1969), p. 164.
29   Ibid., pp. 16–17.
30   Quoted by Maas, ibid., p. 180.
31   J. A. Sutherland, *Victorian Novelists and Publishers* (Chicago, Ill., University of Chicago Press, 1976), p. 25.
32   Ibid., p. 27.
33   Howe, *Geraldine Jewsbury*, pp. 78–80.
34   Ibid., p. 71.
35   Letter to Tottie Fox, quoted in Winifred Gerin, *Elizabeth Gaskell, A Biography* (Oxford, Oxford University Press, 1980), pp. 138–9.
36   C. P. Darcy, *The Encouragement of the Fine Arts in Lancashire 1760–1860* (The Chetham Society, Manchester, 1976), p. 163.
37   Heleniak, *William Mulready*, pp. 168, 137, 138.
38   Ibid., p. 168, and n. 58, pp. 260–1.
39   Maas, *Victorian Painters*, p. 164.
40   E. D. H. Johnson, 'The Making of Ford Madox Brown's "Work" ', in Ira Bruce Nadel and F. S. Schwarzbach (eds), *Victorian Artists and the City* (Oxford, Pergamon Press, 1980), p. 146 (Italics in original.)
41   Frances Borzello, 'Pictures for the People', in Nadel and Schwarzbach (eds), *Victorian Artists and the City*.

42   Ibid., p. 31.
43   Ibid., pp. 36, 37.
44   Ibid., pp. 35–6.
45   Hugh   Cunningham,   *Leisure   in   the   Industrial   Revolution c.1780–c.1880* (London, Croom Helm, 1980), ch. 3; Peter Bailey, *Leisure and Class in Victorian England: Rational Recreation and the Contest for Control 1830–1885* (London, Routledge & Kegan Paul, 1978), pp. 59–60.
46   Cunningham, *Leisure in the Industrial Revolution*, p. 130.
47   Robert Thorne, 'Places of Refreshment in the Nineteenth-Century City' in Anthony D. King (ed.), *Buildings and Society, Essays on the Social Development of the Built Environment* (London, Routledge & Kegan Paul, 1980), p. 235. However, some later restaurants, such as the Criterion Theatre and Restaurant in London, which opened in 1874, did make provision for ladies, offering a place 'where even the most timid of women could eat while visiting the West End'. Ibid., p. 243.
48   Cunningham *Leisure in the Industrial Revolution*, p. 135. See also George Rowell, *The Victorian Theatre 1792–1914* (Cambridge, Cambridge University Press, 1978), pp. 82–4. But even in 1843 Geraldine Jewsbury, on a visit to London, went to the theatre, to see Clara Novello in *Sappho* at Drury Lane; Howe *Geraldine Jewsbury*, pp. 49–50.
49   R.J. Morris, 'Middle-Class Culture, 1700–1914', in Derek Fraser (ed.), *A History of Modern Leeds* (Manchester, Manchester University Press, 1980), p. 217.
50   T.W. Heyck, *The Transformation of Intellectual Life in Victorian England* (London, Croom Helm, 1982), pp. 58–9.
51   Davidoff and Hall, 'Architecture of Public and Private Life', pp. 341–2.
52   Ibid.
53   Thomas S. Ashton, *Economic and Social Investigations in Manchester, 1833–1933*, (Brighton, Harvester Press, 1977), p. 150. The papers were 'On the Prevention of Excessive Infant Mortality' by Mrs M.A. Baines, and 'A Criticism on the Paper read by Dr Pankhurst "On the Exemption of Private Property at Sea from Capture during War" ' by Mrs M. Hamlin.
54   Robert H. Kargon, *Science in Victorian Manchester: Enterprise and Expertise* (Manchester, Manchester University Press, 1977), pp. 194, 209.
55   Stuart Macdonald, *The History and Philosophy of Art Education* (London, University of London Press, 1970), p. 30.
56   Ibid., p. 108.
57   Ibid., p. 146. As Macdonald says, the Schools 'promised a career as a governess or freelance designer to the less fortunate "reduced gentlewomen" or "daughters of decayed tradesmen" '. Ibid., p. 148.
58   Ibid., p. 147.

59   Heleniak, *William Mulready*, pp. 163–4.
60   Rozsika Parker and Griselda Pollock, *Old Mistresses: Women, Art and Ideology* (London, Routledge & Kegan Paul, 1981), p. 54. See also John Seed: ' "Commerce and the Liberal Arts": The Political Economy of Art in Manchester, 1775–1860', in Janet Wolff and John Seed (eds), *The Culture of Capital: Art, Power and the Nineteenth-Century Middle Class* (Manchester, Manchester University Press, 1988).
61   Ibid., pp. 35, 87–90. See also Macdonald, *History and Philosophy of Art Education*, p. 30.
62   Gerin, *Elizabeth Gaskell*, p. 96.
63   Howe, *Geraldine Jewsbury*, pp. 54, 81, 86, 152.
64   Ellen Moers, *Literary Women: The Great Writers* (New York, Doubleday Anchor Press, 1977), p. 64. See also 'The Invisible *Flâneuse*: Women and the Literature of Modernity', included in collection.
65   Tony Davies. 'Transports of Pleasure', *Formations of Pleasure* (London, Routledge & Kegan Paul, 1983), p. 55.
66   Patricia Stubbs, *Women and Fiction. Feminism and the Novel 1880–1920* (Brighton, Harvester Press, 1979), pp. xi–xii.
67   Heleniak, *William Mulready*, p. 147.
68   Rowell, *Victorian Theatre*, p. 109. See also Linda Nochlin, '*Lost and Found*: Once More the Fallen Woman', in Norma Broude and Mary D. Garrard (eds), *Feminism and Art History: Questioning the Litany* (New York, Harper & Row, 1982). For a rather different, more carefully social-historical interpretation of the same theme, see Lynda Nead, 'Seduction, Prostitution, Suicide: *On the Brink* by Alfred Elmore', *Art History*, 5, 3 (September 1982). For a discussion of 'happy mothers' in the rather different context of French eighteenth-century paintings, see Carol Duncan, 'Happy Mothers and Other New Ideas in Eighteenth-Century French Art', also in Broude and Garrard (eds), *Feminism and Art History*.
69   Rosemary Treble, Introduction to *Great Victorian Pictures* (Arts Council of Great Britain, 1978), p. 32.
70   Raymond Williams, 'Forms of English Fiction in 1848', in *Writing in Society* (London, Verso, n.d.), pp. 152–3. (Originally published in Francis Barker *et al.* (eds), *1848: The Sociology of Literature* (Colchester, University of Essex, 1978).)
71   Heleniak, *William Mulready*, pp. 48–50.
72   Steven Marcus, *The Other Victorians: A Study of Sexuality and Pornography in Mid-Nineteenth-Century England* (London, Weidenfeld & Nicolson, 1966).
73   Cunningham, *Leisure in the Industrial Revolution*, pp. 130–1; Robert W. Malcolmson, *Popular Recreations in English Society 1700–1850* (Cambridge, Cambridge University Press, 1973), pp. 76–9.
74   Maas, *Victorian Painters*, p. 169.

75 Jeannie Chapel, *Victorian Taste: The Complete Catalogue of Paintings at the Royal Holloway College* (A Zwemmer, 1982), pp. 108–9.
76 For example, Marxist-Feminist Literature Collective, 'Women's Writing: *Jane Eyre, Shirley, Villette, Aurora Leigh*', *Ideology & Consciousness*, no. 3 (Spring 1978). (Also published in Barker *et al.* (eds.). *1848: The Sociology of Literature*) Also Sandra M. Gilbert and Susan Gubar, *The Madwoman in the Attic: The Woman Writer and the Nineteenth-Century Literary Imagination*, (Cambridge, Mass., Yale University Press, 1979); Annette Kolodny, 'Dancing through the Minefield: Some Observations on the Theory, Practice and Politics of a Feminist Literary Criticism', *Feminist Studies*, 6, 1, (Spring 1980).
77 Caroline Arscott, 'Employer, Husband Spectator: Thomas Fairbairn's Commission of *The Awakening Conscience*', in Wolff and Seed (eds), *The Culture of Capital*.
78 Michel Foucault, *The History of Sexuality Volume One: An Introduction* (Harmondsworth, Penguin, 1981).
79 See E. Ann Kaplan, 'Is the Gaze Male?', in Ann Snitow, Christine Stansell, and Sharon Thompson (eds), *Desire: The Politics of Sexuality* (London, Virago, 1984). See also the essays in Constance Penley (ed.), *Feminism and Film Theory* (London, Routledge, 1988).
80 Lynda Nead, 'Representation, Sexuality and the Female Nude', *Art History*, 6 (1983), p. 236. See also her essays 'Seduction, Prostitution, Suicide: *On the Brink* by Alfred Elmore', *Art History*, 5 (1982), and 'The Magdalen in Modern Times: The Mythology of the Fallen Woman in Pre-Raphaelite Painting', *The Oxford Art Journal*, 7 (1984).

3

The Invisible *Flâneuse*: Women and the Literature of Modernity

The Experience of Modernity

The literature of modernity describes the experience of men. It is essentially a literature about transformations in the public world and in its associated consciousness. The actual date of the advent of 'the modern' varies in different accounts, and so do the characteristics of 'modernity' identified by different writers. But what nearly all the accounts have in common is their concern with the public world of work, politics, and city life. And these are areas from which women were excluded, or in which they were practically invisible. For example, if the chief characteristic of modernity is the Weberian idea of increasing rationalization, then the major institutions affected by this process were the factory, the office, and the government department. There have, of course, always been women working in factories; the growth of bureaucracies was also to some extent dependent on the development of a new female work force of clerks and secretaries. Nevertheless, it is appropriate to talk of this world as a 'male' world for two reasons. First, the institutions were run by men, for men (owners, industrialists, managers, financiers), and they were dominated by men in their operation and hierarchical structure. Secondly, the development of the factory and, later, the bureaucracy coincides with that process, by now well documented, of the 'separation of spheres', and the increasing restriction of women to the 'private' sphere of the home and the suburb.[1] Although lower middle-class and working-class women continued to go out to work throughout the nineteenth century, the ideology of women's place in the domestic realm permeated the whole of society, at least in England, as evidenced by the working-class demand for a 'family wage' for men.[2] The public sphere, then, despite the presence of some women in certain contained areas of it, was a masculine domain. And insofar as the experience of 'the modern' occurred mainly in the public sphere, it was primarily men's experience.

In this essay, however, I shall not pursue the more orthodox sociological analyses of modernity, which discuss the phenomenon in terms of the rationalization process (or perhaps the 'civilizing process' – this, of course, places the event at a much earlier date). I want to consider the more impressionistic and essayistic contributions of those writers who locate the specifically 'modern' in city life: in the fleeting, ephemeral, impersonal nature of encounters in the urban environment, and in the particular world-view which the city-dweller develops. This focus is not foreign to sociology: the essays of Georg Simmel immediately come to mind as studies in the social psychology of city life,[3] and the more recent sociology of Richard Sennett has revived interest in the diagnosis of the modern urban personality.[4] But a particular concern for the experience of modernity has also run through literary criticism; here its early prophet was Charles Baudelaire, the poet of mid-nineteenth-century Paris.[5] Walter Benjamin's essays on Baudelaire, written in the 1930s, provide a fascinating (though typically cryptic and fragmentary) series of reflections on Baudelaire's views on 'the modern'.[6] As a starting-point for the investigation of this particular literature of modernity, I take Baudelaire's statement, in the essay written in 1859–60, *The Painter of Modern Life*: 'By "modernity" I mean the ephemeral, the fugitive, the contingent, the half of art whose other half is the eternal and the immutable.'[7] This is echoed in Marshall Berman's recent book on the experience of modernity, which describes the 'paradoxical unity' of modernity: 'A unity of disunity: it pours us all into a maelstrom of perpetual disintegration and renewal, of struggle and contradiction, of ambiguity and anguish. To be modern is to be part of a universe in which, as Marx said, "all that is solid melts into air" '.[8] It also recalls Simmel's account of the metropolitan personality: 'The psychological basis of the metropolitan type of individuality consists in the *intensification of nervous stimulation* which results from the swift and uninterrupted change of outer and inner stimuli' (Italics in original).[9]

For Simmel, this is closely related to the money economy,

dominant by the late nineteenth century. It is worth stressing that, although cities were not new in the nineteenth century, the critics (and defenders) of modernity believed that urban existence took on an entirely different character around the middle of the nineteenth century. Though any such dating is, to some extent, arbitrary (and will vary, anyway, from Paris to London to Berlin),[10] I think it is useful to take this period of accelerated urbanization, coupled with the transformations in work, housing, and social relations brought about by the rise of industrial capitalism, as the crucial years of the birth of 'modernity'. Berman gives modernity a pre-history, in those elements of the modern which began to appear in the period before the French Revolution and which found their expression in Goethe's *Faust*.[11] Bradbury and McFarlane, who focus on the later period of 1890 to 1930, credit Baudelaire as an 'initiator' of modernism.[12] But they are writing about the rather different phenomenon of modern*ism* in the arts; although 'modernism' and 'modernity' are often conflated, I do not think anyone has claimed that Baudelaire was a modernist poet, in the sense of revoutionizing poetic language and form.[13] There is no contradiction in locating the early experience of 'modernity' in the mid-nineteenth century, and its later expression in the arts at the end of the century.

The peculiar characteristics of modernity, then, consist in the transient and 'fugitive' nature of encounters and impressions made in the city. A sociology of modernity must, ultimately, be able to identify the origins of these new patterns of behaviour and experience, in the social and material aspects of the contemporary society. Simmel, as I have said, relates the metropolitan personality and what he calls the 'blasé attitude' to the money economy. Marshall Berman, beginning from Marx's account of the 'melting vision,'[14] seems to take over at the same time Marx's analysis of the basis of this vision in the radical changes wrought in society by the bourgeoisie and the capitalist mode of production. Baudelaire, on the other hand, considers the phenomenon itself, and not its causes. It is not my task here to provide a sociology of modernity, and so I shall not assess competing accounts of the social or economic base of the modern experience, nor even examine very closely the adequacy of the conceptions of 'modernity' I discuss. What I want to do is to take those accounts, which do describe, more or less sociologically, the modern urban experience, and consider them from the point of view of gender divisions in nineteenth-century society. To that extent, it does not really matter whether a partic-

ular account is adequately grounded in a social-historical understanding of the period, or even whether an account is internally
consistent. (As Berman shows, Baudelaire employs several different
conceptions of 'modernity', as well as changing evaluations of the
phenomenon.[15])

Baudelaire's comments on modernity are most explicit in his
writings on art criticism, though the same themes can be found in
his poetry and in his prose poems. An early reference appears at the
end of his review of *The Salon of 1845*, appended almost as an
afterthought in the final paragraph. Here he commends contemporary painting, but laments its lack of interest in the present.

> No one is cocking his ear to tomorrow's wind; and yet the heroism of
> *modern life* surrounds and presses upon us. We are quite sufficiently
> choked by our true feelings for us to be able to recognize them. There is
> no lack of subjects, nor of colours, to make epics. The painter, the true
> painter for whom we are looking, will be he who can snatch its epic
> quality from the life of today and can make us see and understand, with
> brush or with pencil, how great and poetic we are in our cravats and our
> patent-leather boots. Next year let us hope that the true seekers may
> grant us the extraordinary delight of celebrating the advent of the *new*.[16]

But the following year was no better, and again Baudelaire
bemoans the absence of any really contemporary art, concerned
with modern themes and characters in the way that Balzac's novels
are. This time he devotes several pages – the final section of the
review of *The Salon of 1846* – to the theme of 'the heroism of
modern life'. Modern life here begins to acquire some identifiable
features: the uniform drabness of the colours of people's dress, the
modern phenomenon of the 'dandy' who reacts against this, the
'private subjects' which Baudelaire extols as far more 'heroic' than
the public and official subjects of painting:

> The pageant of fashionable life and the thousands of floating
> existences – criminals and kept women – which drift about in the
> underworld of a great city; the *Gazette des Tribunaux* and the *Moniteur*
> all prove to us that we have only to open our eyes to recognize our
> heroism . . . The life of our city is rich in poetic and marvellous
> subjects.[17]

These subjects are itemized in more detail in *The Painter of
Modern Life* of 1859–60. By this time, Baudelaire has found a

painter he considers equal to the task of depicting the modern: Constantin Guys, the subject of the essay. Guys' watercolours and drawings are generally considered to be talented but superficial works, of little importance in the history of art – though judgements like these do, of course, beg all sorts of questions about critical assessment. Berman dismisses Guys' 'slick renderings of the "beautiful people" and their world' and wonders that Baudelaire should think so highly of an art which 'resembles nothing so much as Bonwit's or Bloomingdale's ads'.[18] Nevertheless, the essay is interesting for its expansion of the notion of 'modernity'. Guys, the 'painter of modern life', goes out into the crowd and records the myriad impressions of day and night.

> He goes and watches the river of life flow past him in all its splendour and majesty . . . He gazes upon the landscapes of the great city – landscapes of stone, caressed by the mist or buffeted by the sun. He delights in fine carriages and proud horses, the dazzling smartness of the grooms, the expertness of the footman, the sinuous gait of the women, the beauty of the children . . . If a fashion or the cut of a garment has been slightly modified, if bows and curls have been supplanted by cockades, if *bavolets* have been enlarged and *chignons* have dropped a fraction towards the nape of the neck, if waists have been raised and skirts have become fuller, be very sure that his eagle eye will already have spotted it from however great a distance.[19]

This is the passage Berman dismisses as 'advertising copy'. But if it is an inventory of the superficial and the merely fashionable, then that is the point – the modern consciousness consists in the parade of impressions, the particular beauty appropriate to the modern age. And, more important, it is in this essay that Baudelaire suggests the formal features of the modern mind, which grasps 'the ephemeral, the fugitive, the contingent'. The dandy appears again, to be compared and also contrasted with Guys, similar in their concern for appearance and for personal originality, divided by the blasé and insensitive attitude of the former which Guys (according to Baudelaire[20]) abhors. Guys is the *flâneur*, in his element in the crowd – at the centre of the world and at the same time hidden from the world.[21]

The *flâneur* – the stroller – is a central figure in Benjamin's essays on Baudelaire and nineteenth-century Paris. The streets and arcades of the city are the home of the *flâneur*, who, in Benjamin's phrase, 'goes botanizing on the asphalt'.[22] The anonymity of the crowd provides an asylum for the person on the margins of society; here Benjamin includes both Baudelaire himself as a *flâneur*, and the victims and murderers of Poe's detective stories (which Baudelaire translated into French).[23] For Benjamin, however, the city of the *flâneur* is historically more limited than for Baudelaire. Neither London nor Berlin offers precisely the conditions of involvement/non-involvement in which the Parisian *flâneur* flourishes; nor does the Paris of a slightly later period, when a 'network of controls' has made escape into anonymity impossible.[24] (Baudelaire, and Berman, on the contrary argue that the Paris increasingly opened up by Haussmann's boulevards, which broke down the social and geographical divisions between the classes, is even more the site of the modern gaze, the ambit of the *flâneur*).[25]

The *flâneur* is the modern hero; his experience, like that of Guys, is that of a freedom to move about in the city, observing and being observed, but never interacting with others. A related figure in the literature of modernity is the *stranger*. One of Baudelaire's prose poems, *Paris Spleen*, is entitled *L'étranger*.[26] It is a short dialogue, in which an 'enigmatic man' is asked what or whom he loves – his father, mother, sister, brother? his friends, his country, beauty, gold? To all of these he answers in the negative, affirming that he simply loves the passing clouds. For Simmel, the stranger is not a man without attachments and involvements, however. He is characterized by a particular kind of 'inorganic' membership of the group, not having been a member from its beginning, but having settled down in a new place. He is 'the person who comes today and stays tomorrow';[27] in this he differs from both the *flâneur* and Baudelaire's *étranger*, neither of whom will settle down or even make contact with those around him. But Simmel's stranger is always a 'potential wanderer': 'Although he has not moved on, he has not quite overcome the freedom of coming and going'.[28] These heroes of modernity thus share the possibility and the prospect of lone travel, of voluntary uprooting, of anonymous arrival at a new place. They are, of course, all men.

Women and Public Life

It is no accident, and no fault of a careless patriarchal use of language, that Richard Sennett's book on modernity is called *The Fall of Public* **Man**. The 'public' person of the eighteenth century and earlier, whose demise is charted, and who passed the time in coffee-houses, paraded in the streets and at the theatre, and addressed strangers freely in public places, was clearly male. (Although Sennett says that it was quite proper to address strange women in the parks or the street, as long as men did not thereby assume that a reply meant they might call on the woman at home, there is no suggestion that *women* might address strangers.[29]) In the nineteenth-century city, no longer the arena of that public life, the *flâneur* makes his appearance – to be watched, but not addressed.[30] Men and women may have shared the privatization of personality, the careful anonymity and withdrawal in public life; but the line drawn increasingly sharply between the public and private was also one which confined women to the private, while men retained the freedom to move in the crowd or to frequent cafés and pubs. The men's clubs replaced the coffee-houses of earlier years.

None of the authors I have discussed is unaware of the different experience of women in the modern city. Sennett, for example, recognizes that '(the) right to escape to public privacy was unequally enjoyed by the sexes', since even by the late nineteenth century, women could not go alone to a café in Paris or a restaurant in London.[31] As he says: ' "The lonely crowd" was a realm of privatized freedom, and the male, whether simply out of domination or greater need, was more likely to escape in it'. He notes, too, that in the earlier period of 'public life' women had to take a good deal more care about the 'signs' of their dress, which would be scrutinized for an indication of their social rank; in the nineteenth century, the scrutiny would be in order to differentiate 'respectable' from 'loose' women.[32] Simmel, whose essayistic sociology I have used very selectively, also paid much attention elsewhere to the condition of women. He wrote essays on the position of women, the psychology of women, female culture, and the women's movement and social democracy.[33] He was one of the first to permit women in his private seminars, long before they were admitted as full students at the University of Berlin.[34] Berman, too, considers women, acknowledging somewhat belatedly (on page 322 of his book) that they have a totally different experience of the city from that of men. He suggests that Jane Jacobs's *The Death and Life of Great American Cities* gives a 'fully articulated woman's view of the city'.[35] Published in 1961, Jacobs's book describes her own daily life in the city – a life of neighbours, shopkeepers, and young children, as well as work. The importance of the book, says Berman,[36] is that it reveals that 'women had something to tell us about the city and the life we shared, and that we had impoverished our own lives as well as theirs by not listening to them till now'.

The problem is, though, that it is also the literature of modernity which has been impoverished by ignoring the lives of women. The dandy, the *flâneur*, the hero, the stranger – all figures invoked to epitomize the experience of modern life – are invariably male figures. In 1831, when George Sand wanted to experience Paris life and to learn about the ideas and arts of her time, she dressed as a boy, to give herself the freedom she knew women could not share:

> So I had made for myself a *redingote-guérite* in heavy gray cloth, pants and vest to match. With a gray hat and large woollen cravat, I was a perfect first-year student. I can't express the pleasure my boots gave me: I would gladly have slept with them, as my brother did in his young age, when he got his first pair. With those little iron-shod heels, I was solid on the pavement. I flew from one end of Paris to the other. It seemed to me that I could go round the world. And then, my clothes feared nothing. I ran out in every kind of weather, I came home at every sort of hour, I sat in the pit at the theatre. No one paid attention to me, and no one guessed at my disguise . . . No one knew me, no one looked at me, no one found fault with me; I was an atom lost in that immense crowd.[37]

The disguise made the life of the *flâneur* available to her; as she knew very well, she could not adopt the non-existent role of a *flâneuse*. Women could not stroll alone in the city.

In Baudelaire's essays and poems, women appear very often. Modernity breeds, or makes visible, a number of categories of female city-dwellers. Among those most prominent in these texts are: the prostitute, the widow, the old lady, the lesbian, the murder victim, and the passing unknown woman. Indeed, according to Benjamin, the lesbian was for Baudelaire the heroine of modernism; certainly it is known that he originally intended to give the title *Les Lesbiennes* to the poems which became *Les Fleurs du Mal*.[38] Yet, as Benjamin also points out, in the major poem about lesbians of the series, *Delphine et Hippolyte*, Baudelaire concludes by condemning the women as 'lamentable victims', bound for hell.[39] The prostitute, the subject of the poem *Crépuscule du Soir* and also discussed in a section of *The Painter of Modern Life*, elicits a similarly ambivalent attitude of admiration and disgust (the poem comparing prostitution to an anthill, and to a worm stealing a man's food).[40] More unequivocal is Baudelaire's sympathy for those other marginal women, the old woman and the widow; the former he 'watches tenderly from afar' like a father, the latter he observes with a sensitivity to her pride, pain, and poverty.[41] But none of these women meet the poet as his equal. They are subjects of his gaze, objects of his 'botanising'. The nearest he comes to a direct encounter, with a woman who is not either marginal or debased, is in the poem, *À Une Passante*.[42] (Even here, it is worth noting that the woman in question is in mourning – *en grand deuil*.) The tall, majestic woman passes him in the busy street; their eyes meet for a moment before she continues her journey, and the poet remains to ask whether they will only meet again in eternity. Her return of his gaze is confirmed in the last line: 'O toi que j'eusse aimée, o toi qui le savais'. Benjamin's interpretation of this poem is that it is the very elusiveness of the passing encounter that fascinates Baudelaire: 'The delight of the city-dweller is not so much love at first sight as love at last sight'.[43] The meeting is characterized by the peculiarly modern feature of 'shock'.[44] (But if this is the rare exception of a woman sharing the urban experience, we may also ask whether a 'respectable' woman in the 1850s would have met the gaze of a strange man.)

There is, in any case, an apparently common assumption that women who do participate in 'the public' on anything like the same terms as men somehow manifest masculine traits. One of the widows observed by Baudelaire is described as having mannerisms of a masculine character.[45] His mixed admiration for the lesbian has much to do with her (supposed) 'mannishness', according to Benjamin.[46] Benjamin himself explains that, as women in the nineteenth century had to go out to work in factories, 'in the course of time masculine traits were bound to manifest themselves in these women'.[47] Even Richard Sennett (without much evidence, and despite the benefit of contemporary perspectives on the construction of gender) claims that women at the end of the nineteenth century who were 'ideologically committed to emancipation' dressed like men and developed bodily gestures which were 'mannish'.[48] But perhaps this perception of the 'masculine' in woman who were visible in a man's world is only the displaced recognition of women's overall exclusion from that world. Baudelaire's general views on women, in his letters and his prose, are illuminating as a context for his poetic expressions of fascination with 'women of the city'. This is his own admission, in a letter to one of the women he idolized and idealized: 'I have hateful prejudices about women. In fact, *I have no faith*; you have a fine soul, but, when all is said, it is the soul of a woman'.[49] Woman as non-person is extolled in *The Painter of Modern Life*:

> Woman, in a word, for the artist in general, and Monsieur G in partic-ular, is far more than just the female of Man. Rather she is a divinity, a star, which presides at all the conceptions of the brain of man; a glittering conglomeration of all the graces of Nature, condensed into a single being; the object of the keenest admiration and curiosity that the picture of life can offer its contemplator. She is a kind of idol, stupid perhaps, but dazzling and bewitching, who holds wills and destinies suspended on her glance . . . Everything that adorns woman, every-thing that serves to show off her beauty, is part of herself, and those artists who have made a particular study of this enigmatic being dote no less on all the details of the *mundus muliebris* than on Woman herself . . . What poet, in sitting down to paint the pleasure caused by the sight of a beautiful woman, would venture to separate her from her costume.[50]

The classic misogynist duality, of woman as idealized-but-vapid/real-and-sensual-but-detested, which Baudelaire displays (and to which his biographers attest) is clearly related to the partic-ular parade of women we observe in this literature of modernity.

But the other authors I have discussed were not misogynists; they were or are, on the contrary, sympathetic to women's condition and to the cause of women's emancipation and equality with men. We need to look deeper than particular prejudices to explain the invisibility of women in the literature of modernity. The explana-tion is three-fold, and lies in (1) the nature of sociological investiga-tion, (2) the consequently partial conception of 'modernity', and (3) the reality of women's place in society. Much of this has been discussed in the recent work of feminist sociologists and historians, but it is worth rehearsing here in the specific context of the problem of modernity.

The Invisibility of Women in the Literature of Modernity

The rise and development of sociology in the nineteenth century was closely related to the growth and increasing separation of 'public' and 'private' spheres of activity in western industrial societies. The condition for this was the separation of work from home, with the development of factories and offices. By the mid-nineteenth century, this had made possible the move to the suburbs in some major cities (for example, the industrial cities of England, like Manchester and Birmingham).[51] Although women had never been engaged on equal terms (financial, legal, or otherwise) with men, this physical separation put an end to their close and important involvement in what had often been a family concern – whether in trade, production, or even professional work. Their gradual confinement to the domestic world of the home and the suburb was strongly reinforced by an ideology of separate spheres.[52] At the same time, a new public world was in process of formation, of business organizations, political and financial establishments, and social and cultural institutions. These were almost invariably male institutions, though women might occasionally be granted some sort of honorary membership or allowed minimal participation as guests on particular occasions. In the second half of the century the rise of the professions excluded women from other expanding areas of activity, some of which they had traditionally been engaged in (like medicine), some of which had already excluded them (like the law and academic occupations), and some of which were new (the education of artists, for example). The two major implications for sociology as a new discipline were, first, that it was dominated by men, and second, that it was primarily concerned with the 'public' spheres of work, politics, and the market place.[53] Indeed, women appear in the classic texts of sociology only insofar as they relate to men, in the family, or in minor roles in the public sphere. As David Morgan has said about Weber's *The Protestant Ethic and the Spirit of Capitalism*: 'It cannot have escaped many people's attention, at least in recent years, that women are very much hidden from this particular history; the lead parts – Franklin, Luther, Calvin, Baxter and Wesley – are all played by men and women only appear on the stage fleetingly in the guise of German factory workers with rather traditional orientations to work.'[54]

To some extent the 'separation of spheres' was an incomplete process, since many women still had to go to work to earn a living (though a very high proportion of these did so in domestic service); but even these women, in their factories, mills, schools, and offices, have been invisible in traditional sociological texts. The public institutions in which they did participate were rarely those accorded most importance by analysts of contemporary society.

This also meant that the particular experience of 'modernity' was, for the most part, equated with experience *in* the public arena. The accelerated growth of the city, the shock of the proximity of the very rich and the destitute poor (documented by Engels – and in some cities avoided and alleviated by the creation of suburbs), and the novelty of the fleeting and impersonal contacts in public life, provided the concern and the fascination for the authors of 'the modern', sociologists and other social commentators who documented their observations in academic essays, literary prose, or poetry. To some extent, of course, these transformations of social life affected everyone, regardless of sex and class, though they did so differently for different groups. But the literature of modernity ignores the private sphere, and to that extent is silent on the subject of women's primary domain. This silence is not only detrimental to any understanding of the lives of the female sex; it obscures a crucial part of the lives of men, too, by abstracting one part of their experience and failing to explore the interrelation of public and private spheres. For men inhabited both of these. Moreover, the public could only be constituted as a particular set of institutions and practices on the basis of the removal of other areas of social life to the invisible arena of the private.[55] The literature of modernity, like most sociology of its period, suffers from what has recently been called 'the oversocialisation of the public sphere'.[56] The skewed vision of its authors explains why women only appear in this literature through their relationships with men in the public sphere, and via their illegitimate or eccentric routes into this male arena – that is, in the role of whore, widow, or murder victim.[57]

The real situation of women in the second half of the nineteenth century was more complex than one of straightforward confinement to the home. It varied from one social class to another, and even from one geographical region to another, depending on the local industry, the degree of industrialization, and numerous other factors. And, although the solitary and independent life of the *flâneur* was not open to women, women clearly *were* active and visible in other ways in the public arena. Sennett, as I have already mentioned, refers to the importance of careful attention to dress which women must maintain, a point made much earlier by Thorstein Veblen:

It has in the course of economic development become the office of the woman to consume vicariously for the head of the household; and her apparel is contrived with this object in view. It has come about that obviously productive labor is in a peculiar degree derogatory to respectable women, and therefore special pains should be taken in the construction of women's dress, to impress upon the beholder the fact (often indeed a fiction) that the wearer does not and can not habitually engage in useful work.[58]

Here, the particular visibility of women is as sign of their husbands' position. Their important role in consumption is stressed:

At the stage of economic development at which the women were still in the full sense the property of the men, the performance of conspicuous leisure and consumption came to be part of the services required of them. The women being not their own masters, obvious expenditure and leisure on their part would redound to the credit of their master rather than to their own credit; and therefore the more expensive and the more obviously unproductive the women of the household are, the more creditable and more effective for the purpose of reputability of the household or its head will their life be.[59]

The establishment of the department store in the 1850s and 1860s provided an important new arena for the legitimate public appearance of middle-class women.[60] However, although consumerism is a central aspect of modernity, and moreover mediated the public/private division, the peculiar characteristics of 'the modern' which I have been considering – the fleeting, anonymous encounter and the purposeless strolling – do not apply to shopping, or to women's activities either as public signs of their husband's wealth or as consumers.

We are beginning to find out more about the lives of women who were limited to the domestic existence of the suburbs;[61] about women who went into domestic service in large numbers;[62] and about the lives of working-class women.[63] The advent of the modern era affected all these women, transforming their experience of home and work. The recovery of women's experience is part of the project of retrieving what has been hidden, and attempting to fill the gaps in the classic accounts. The feminist revision of sociology and social history means the gradual opening up of areas of social life and experience which to date have been obscured by the partial perspective and particular bias of mainstream sociology.

It is not at all clear what a feminist sociology of modernity would look like. There is no question of inventing the *flâneuse*: the essential point is that such a character was rendered impossible by the sexual divisions of the nineteenth century. Nor is it appropriate to reject totally the existing literature on modernity, for the experiences it describes certainly defined a good deal of the lives of men, and were also (but far less centrally) a part of the experience of women. What is missing in this literature is any account of life outside the public realm, of the experience of 'the modern' in its private manifestations, and also of the very different nature of the experience of those women who *did* appear in the public arena: a poem written by 'la femme passante' about her encounter with Baudelaire, perhaps.

NOTES

This essay was written during a period of research leave, funded by the ESRC in connection with a larger project investigating nineteenth-century middle-class culture. The ideas developed here, while not central to that project, draw on work done in relation to that research.

1　Catherine Hall, 'Gender Divisions and Class Formation in the Birmingham Middle Class, 1780–1850', in Raphael Samuel (ed.), *People's History and Socialist Theory* (London, Routledge & Kegan Paul, 1981); and Leonore Davidoff and Catherine Hall, 'The Architecture of Public and Private Life: English Middle-Class Society in a Provincial Town 1780–1850', in D. Fraser and A. Sutcliffe (eds), *The Pursuit of Urban History* (London, Edward Arnold, 1983).

2　Hilary Land, 'The Family Wage', *Feminist Review*, 6 (1980); and Michèle Barrett and Mary McIntosh, 'The "Family Wage": Some Problems for Socialists and Feminists', *Capital & Class*, 11 (1980). The ideology of separate spheres, and even of the equation of male/public/rational has persisted to the present day, its recent sociological expression being found in Parsonian theories of the family. (See Talcott Parsons, 'Family Structure and the Socialization of the Child', in Talcott Parsons and Robert F. Bales, *Family, Socialization and Interaction Process* (London, Routledge & Kegan Paul, 1956.)

3　George Simmel, 'The Stranger' and 'The Metropolis and Mental Life', in Kurt H. Wolff (ed.), *The Sociology of George Simmel* (New York, Free Press, 1950).

4　Richard Sennett, *The Fall of Public Man* (Cambridge, Cambridge University Press, 1974).

5　Charles Baudelaire, 'The Painter of Modern Life', in *The Painter of Modern Life and Other Essays*, tr. and ed. Jonathan Mayne (1863;

Oxford, Phaidon Press, 1964). For Baudelaire's other writings on modernity, see below.

6 Walter Benjamin, *Charles Baudelaire: A Lyric Poet in the Era of High Capitalism* (London, New Left Books, 1973).

7 Baudelaire, 'Painter of Modern Life', p. 13.

8 Marshall Berman, *All That Is Solid Melts into Air: The Experience of Modernity* (London, Verso, 1983), p. 15.

9 Simmel, 'Metropolis and Mental Life', pp. 409–10.

10 Benjamin, for example, argues that conditions in the three cities were significantly different (*Charles Baudelaire*, pp. 128–31).

11 Berman, *All That Is Solid Melts into Air*, pp. 16–17 and ch. 1.

12 Malcolm Bradbury and James McFarlane, 'The Name and Nature of Modernism', in Malcolm Bradbury and James McFarlane (eds), *Modernism 1890–1930* (Harmondsworth, Penguin, 1976), p. 36.

13 For example Joanna Richardson, translator of Baudelaire's poems, says in her introduction to *Baudelaire: Selected Poems* (Harmondsworth, Penguin, 1975, p. 20): '*Les Fleurs du Mal* may not be technically original. The only poem in which Baudelaire really seems to have invented his rhythm is *L'invitation au voyage*. His one revolutionary innovation is in the versification, it is the complete suppression of the auditive caesura in a certain number of lines'.

14 The title of his book, *All That Is Sold Melts into Air*, is a quotation from the *Communist Manifesto*.

15 Berman, *All That Is Solid Melts into Air*, pp. 133–42.

16 Baudelaire, 'The Salon of 1845', in *Art in Paris 1845–1862* (Oxford, Phaidon, 1965), pp. 31–2.

17 Baudelaire, 'The Salon of 1846', in *Art in Paris 1845–1862*, pp. 118–19.

18 Berman, *All That Is Solid Melts into Air*, p. 136.

19 Baudelaire, 'Painter of Modern Life', p. 11.

20 Ibid., pp. 9 and 26–9.

21 Ibid., p. 9.

22 Benjamin, *Charles Baudelaire*, p. 36.

23 Ibid., pp. 40, 170. Elsewhere, however, Benjamin argues that Baudelaire is *not* the archetypical *flâneur* (ibid., p. 69).

24 Ibid., pp. 49, 128, 47.

25 Berman, *All That Is Solid Melts into Air*, pp. 150–5.

26 Baudelaire, *Petits poèmes en prose (Le Spleen de Paris)* (Paris, Garnier-Flammarion, 1967), p. 33.

27 Simmel, 'The Stranger', p. 402.

28 Ibid.

29 Sennett, *Fall of Public Man*, p. 86.

30 Ibid., pp. 125, 213.

31 Ibid., p. 217. However, there were exceptions to this (see Robert Thorne, 'Places of Refreshment in the Nineteenth-Century City', in Anthony D. King (ed.), *Buildings and Society, Essays on the Social*

Development of the Built Environment (London, Routledge & Kegan Paul, 1980), p. 243).

32 Sennett, *Fall of Public Man*, pp. 68, 166. In these references to Sennett's book, I am again considering fairly uncritically (from any other point of view) a text on modernity. For a critical review of his use of evidence, his historical method, and his sociological explanation for the changes in manners, see Sheldon Wolin, 'The Rise of Private Man', *New York Review of Books* (14 April 1977).

33 David Frisby, *Sociological Impressionism. A Reassessment of Georg Simmel's Social Theory* (London, Heinemann, 1981), pp. 15, 17, 27, 139.

34 Ibid., p. 28.

35 Berman, *All That Is Solid Melts into Air*, p. 322.

36 Ibid., p. 323.

37 Quoted in Ellen Moers, *Literary Women: The Great Writers* (New York, Doubleday Anchor Press, 1977), p. 12.

38 Benjamin, *Charles Baudelaire*, p. 90; Richardson, Introduction to *Baudelaire*, p. 12.

39 Benjamin, p. 92–3; Baudelaire, *Selected Poems*, p. 224.

40 Baudelaire, *Petits poèmes en prose*, p. 185; *Painter of Modern Life*, pp. 34–40.

41 Baudelaire, *Selected Poems*, p. 166; *Petits poèmes en prose*, pp. 63–5.

42 Baudelaire, *Selected Poems*, p. 170.

43 Benjamin, *Charles Baudelaire*, p. 45.

44 Ibid., p. 125; also pp. 118, 134.

45 Baudelaire, *Petits poèmes en prose*, p. 64.

46 Benjamin, *Charles Baudelaire*, p. 90.

47 Ibid., p. 93.

48 Sennett, *Fall of Public Man*, p. 190.

49 Letter to Apollonie Sabatier, quoted in Richardson, Introduction to *Baudelaire*, p. 14. (Italics in original.)

50 Baudelaire, *Painter of Modern Life*, pp. 30–1.

51 Maurice Spiers, *Victoria Park Manchester* (Manchester, Manchester University Press, 1976); Davidoff and Hall, 'Architecture of Public and Private Life'.

52 Catherine Hall, 'The Early Formation of Victorian Domestic Ideology', in Sandra Burman (ed.), *Fit Work for Women* (London, Croom Helm, 1979).

53 Margaret Stacey, 'The Division of Labour Revisited or Overcoming the Two Adams', in Philip Abrams et al. (eds), *Practice and Progress: British Sociology 1950–80 (London, Allen & Unwin, 1981)*; Sara Delamont, *The Sociology of Women* (London, Allen & Unwin, 1980), ch. 1.

54 David Morgan, 'Men, Masculinity and the Process of Sociological Enquiry', in Helen Roberts (ed.), *Doing Feminist Research* (London, Routledge & Kegan Paul, 1981), p. 93.

55   Sennett does discuss, in passing, some changes in the home – for example the development of the 'private' form of dress – but his central focus is on the public sphere, and he does not present a systematic account of the private or of the relationship between the two spheres (*Fall of Public Man*, pp. 66–7).

56   Eva Gamarnikow and June Purvis, Introduction to Eva Gamarnikow et al. (eds), *The Public and the Private* (London, Heinemann, 1983), p. 2.

57   References to the murder victim, whom I have not discussed, originate in Poe's detective stories, which greatly influenced Baudelaire (see Benjamin, *Charles Baudelaire*, pp. 42–4.

58   Thorstein Veblen, *The Theory of the Leisure Class* (1899; London, Unwin 1970), p. 126.

59   Ibid., pp. 126–7.

60   Thorne, 'Places of Refreshment in the Nineteenth-Century', p. 236.

61   Davidoff and Hall, 'The Architecture of Public and Private Life'; and Catherine Hall, 'The Butcher, the Baker, the Candlestick-Maker: The Shop and the Family in the Industrial Revolution', in Elizabeth Whitelegg et al. (eds), *The Changing Experience of Women* (Oxford, Martin Robertson, 1982).

62   Leonore Davidoff, 'Mastered for Life: Servant and Wife in Victorian and Edwardian England', *Journal of Social History*, 7, 4 (1974).

63   Ivy Pinchbeck, *Women Workers and the Industrial Revolution 1750–1850* (1930; London, Frank Cass, 1977); and Sally Alexander, 'Women's Work in Nineteenth-Century London. A Study of the Years 1820–50', in Juliet Mitchell and Ann Oakley (eds), *The Rights and Wrongs of Women* (Harmondsworth, Penguin, 1976), and in Whitelegg et al. (eds), *Changing Experience of Women*.

4

Feminism and Modernism

In or about December, 1910, human character changed.

Virginia Woolf[1]

Modernity entails a certain valorization of the feminine.

Alice Jardine[2]

Virginia Woolf was, of course, a great champion of the moderns. The quotation is taken from her essay 'Mr Bennett and Mrs Brown' written in 1924, in which she celebrates 'the sound of breaking and falling, crashing and destruction . . . the prevailing sound of the Georgian age'.[3] She contrasts the old-fashioned, long-winded, and contorted passages of description of the Edwardian novelists, particularly in Arnold Bennett's work, with the promise of the new writers to engage directly with character. James Joyce, T.S. Eliot, D.H. Lawrence, E.M. Forster, Lytton Strachey, and (implicitly) Virginia Woolf herself – the 'Georgians' – recognizing that 'the tools of one generation are useless for the next',[4] began the task of creating a literature to suit the age.

But why December 1910? Virginia Woolf goes on to say that the change was not sudden and definite, adding only 'since one must be arbitrary, let us date it about the year 1910'.[5] The death of King Edward VII and accession of George V in that year is clearly the central symbolic event. But perhaps even more important was the first Post-Impressionist exhibition held in London. This was organized by Virginia Woolf's friend, Roger Fry, and it represented the first serious introduction into Britain of modernist painting from the continent. The date thus conjoins the aesthetic and the

political, explaining the real significance of Woolf's literary categories of 'Edwardians' and 'Georgians'.

Virginia Woolf's feminist sympathies are well known, her essays
A Room of One's Own and *Three Guineas* revived by contemporary
feminism as still-topical and illuminating comments on the situation
of women in literature, politics, and social life. In some of her
literary critical essays, which are less widely read, she addresses the
question of women's writing. For her, the 'change in human
character' and in literature seemed to offer real possibilities for
women to break away from what she describes as 'the sentence
made by men' – loose, heavy, pompous. The woman writer, she
says, must make her own sentence, 'altering and adapting the
current sentence until she writes one that takes the natural shape of
her thought without crushing or distorting it'.[6] She identifies such a
development in the writing of her contemporary, Dorothy
Richardson.

> She has invented, or, if she has not invented, developed and applied to
> her own use, a sentence which we might call the psychological sentence
> of the feminine gender. It is of a more elastic fibre than the old, capable
> of stretching to the extreme, of suspending the frailest particles, of
> enveloping the vaguest shapes.[7]

Women, unable to articulate their specific experiences and
perspective in the world in a language formed and moulded by the
dominant group, men, might now have the opportunity of working
with the new, barely formulated literary and linguistic tools to
speak for themselves.

In this essay I want to look at the relationship between
modernism and feminism. Other feminists since Virginia Woolf
have suggested that the revolution in the arts around the turn of this
century offered exciting opportunities for women writers and
artists, and that the death of realism meant the fragmentation of
patriarchal culture. Sandra Gilbert and Susan Gubar have argued
that modernism can be seen as a product of late nineteenth-century
feminism, its texts to be read as a battle of the sexes.[8] Alice Jardine,
quoted at the beginning of this essay, claims that modernism
allowed the 'putting of women into discourse'.[9] Julia Kristeva's
study of the 'revolution in poetic language' has been taken up by
feminists inspired by her suggestion that avant-garde writing in late
nineteenth-century France articulates the 'semiotic' (that is, the pre-

Symbolic) which predates the child's entry into language and into patriarchy.[10] And in the visual arts, feminist critics have proposed the continuing radical potential for women of a modernist art practice.[11]

I shall come back to some of these arguments later. However their very diversity should warn against simplistic assertions and alert us to the complexities in this area. One of the issues to be clarified is the concept of 'modernism' itself. Most of those I have just cited date this at the turn of the century; but others are talking about the period of so-called high modernism (post-Second World War), as well as the *continuing* modernist tradition in the arts (those practices in architecture, dance, painting, and so on which resist the eclecticism, populism, and superficiality of the 'postmodern'). Perry Anderson has pointed out that 'a wide variety of very diverse – indeed incompatible – aesthetic practices' are concealed beneath the label 'modernism', including cubism, futurism, symbolism, constructivism, expressionism, surrealism, and others.[12] Noting, too, that the term covers a range of dates and places, and that unlike the terms 'Baroque', 'Romantic', and 'Neo-Classical' it does not designate a describable object in its own right, he concludes that 'modern*ism* as a notion is the emptiest of all cultural categories'.[13] It will be important, therefore, to clarify the different senses in which the term is used in the debates about feminism and modernism.

It should also be noted that the various arguments for modernism depend on rather different theories – both theories of gender and theories of representation. These range from Kristeva's and Jardine's post-structuralist / psychoanalytic perspectives to the more simplistic reading of literature as direct expression of social reality found in Gilbert and Gubar's work. Nevertheless, I believe it is worthwhile to pursue the question of the congruence of modernism and feminism, and I shall want to argue that modernism (carefully defined) had and continues to have critical and radical potential for women writers and artists.

Books on modernism usually take the period 1890 to 1930 as covering the major transformations of social and philosophical thought, aesthetic codes and practices, and scientific theory which have constituted our modern consciousness.[14] Some vary by a decade or so[15], and others trace the early history or prehistory of modernism.[16] The trajectory of modernism after mid-century is more energetically disputed, however, with regard both to its continued aesthetic and political radicalism as against its apparent incorporation into the institutions and values of capitalist society; and to its specific relationship to postmodernism (precursor, moribund parent, ally, competitor, etc.). For the moment I shall confine myself to the period of early modernism, around 1890 to 1930.

Given the great variety of movements, media, locations, and political affiliations involved, how might we define 'modernism'? Eugene Lunn offers a useful set of characteristics as the key features of this phenomenon, understood as a set of 'multiple revolts against traditional realism and romanticism'.[17] These are: (i) aesthetic self-consciousness or self-reflexiveness; (ii) simultaneity, juxtaposition, or montage; (iii) paradox, ambiguity, and uncertainty; (iv) 'dehumanisation' and the demise of the integrated individual subject or personality.[18] (It might be noted that these features of the 'modern' are strikingly similar to those often identified in the 1980s as the 'postmodern', though the relationship between the two is outside the range of discussion of this essay.) With this cluster of traits identifying a diverse set of anti-realist aesthetic practices, we can consider the proposal that modernism offered particular opportunities for feminist cultural and political interventions.

A glance at the standard histories of modernism is not very encouraging. Like all histories of art, they are stories about men's achievements, in which women barely figure. H. Stuart Hughes's book, *Consciousness and Society*, which reviews the 'reorientation of European social thought' in the period 1890 to 1930, discusses the work of social thinkers, philosophers, psychoanalysts, and writers.[19] The book deals with twenty-four men and no women. Alan Bullock, in an essay which traces the origins of modernism, and catalogues its achievements in the arts, sciences, and social thought, lists one hundred and twenty modern innovators, of whom only four are women: one in literature (Gertrude Stein), two in dance (Isadora Duncan and Pavlova), and one in science (Marie Curie).[20] In his study of American writing in the twenties, Frederick Hoffman includes only seventeen women in the one hundred and thirty four entries in his biographical appendix.[21] It does not look as though modernism was a movement in which women participated very actively. Most people would find it difficult to think quickly of women modernist writers, for example, apart from (perhaps) Virginia Woolf.

As recent feminist studies have shown, this absence of women from the modernist canon is another example of the exclusionary tactics of literary and art history, whereby women writers and artists are somehow written out of the account. Shari Benstock has studied the lives and work of women writers in Paris in the first forty years of this century, and explains their relative obscurity. 'Women's contributions to the modernist literary movement have been doubly suppressed by history, either forgotten by the standard literary histories of this time or rendered inconsequential by memoirs and literary biographies.'[22] Her study reinstates writers like H.D., Gertrude Stein, Djuna Barnes, and Natalie Barney and the publisher Sylvia Beach. Gillian Hanscombe and Virginia L. Smyers, looking at 'the modernist women' from 1910 to 1940, contribute to this work of retrieval.[23] Their subjects are H.D., Bryher, Dorothy Richardson, Amy Lowell, Djuna Barnes, Mary Butts, and Mina Loy. The rediscovery of women writers, a continuing project of feminist criticism, thus begins the task of rewriting the history of modernism. It complements the work of feminist presses over the past couple of decades in republishing work by women which has long been out of print.

In the visual arts, feminist historians have already provided us with many texts about the 'hidden heritage' of those women artists whom mainstream art history has obliterated from the record.[24] More recently some of them have turned their attention to women and modernism. As in literature, the orthodox account of the history of modernism consists of a long list of the names of men. The official lineage begins with Manet or Cézanne, moves through Picasso, Mondrian, Man Ray, Dali, and others, and culminates in the institutionalized, mid-twentieth-century modernism of Jackson Pollock. Now we are beginning to know more about late nineteenth-century women painters like Suzanne Valadon, Mary Cassatt, and Berthe Morisot, marginalized in most histories of Impressionism and French painting.[25] Books and exhibitions about Surrealism have reintroduced Leonor Fini, Frida Kahlo, Lee Miller, and Leonora Carrington to their proper place in the history of this movement.[26] In the history of early twentieth-century German painting, Käthe Kollwitz and Paula Modersohn-Becker are better known than they once were. And women involved in painting at the moment of 'high modernism', like Lee Krasner, are beginning to receive the attention so far denied them while their husbands and male associates were exhibited, fêted, and recorded for posterity.[27]

This task of rediscovering women artists in history has always been an essential one for feminist criticism. However, it has two serious limitations. In the first place, it is clear that in important ways it has made very little difference to the major institutions of publishing, exhibiting, criticism, and teaching insofar as they continue to (re)produce a distorted history of modernism. The growing body of knowledge about women is confined to women's studies courses and texts. Moreover, the official culture persists in focusing on the work of men; the important 1981 exhibition of international work at the Royal Academy in London, *A New Spirit in Painting*, showed the work of thirty-six men and no women. Griselda Pollock has demonstrated the dependence of modernism on the notion of the *male* creative artist[28], and it is clear that the feminist critique of the establishment has more to contend with than a biased history of art. As Andreas Huyssen points out, modernism is always characterized as *masculine* (against the 'feminine' mass culture)[29]. In other words, a necessary task will be to dismantle a particular ideology of modernism.

Secondly, feminist historians must not ignore the fact that art history is not entirely to blame for the marginalization of women. It is equally important to look at the social processes which operated to the disadvantage of women painters in the modern period, and which also explain their relative absence from cultural production. In every period in the history of the arts there have been particular practices and ideologies which have been obstacles to women's participation. By the late nineteenth century, exclusion from the life-class and from membership of the academies was no longer the issue. Nor was participation by writers in the public (male) world of the coffee-house. What were the specific features of cultural life in that period which worked to women's disadvantage?

Shari Benstock suggests that the central themes of modernist writing were bound to marginalize women, whose experience was not encapsulated therein. In particular she identifies the First World War as a major theme, and the post-war psychology of despair as a grounding for the literary movement.[30] But this idea of modernism, as she points out, automatically privileges the masculine experience. Women's different perspective on the war was seen as secondary, since they did not write about the trenches, the activism and involvement, the proximity of death. Nor did they experience the male bonding produced by the war, seen by some writers as central to modernism. So women's writing of the period, much of it at least as innovative as that of men, simply does not *count* as 'modernist', given a particular definition of that category. For modernism is conceived as much in terms of its content as in terms of its literary and formal characteristics. Huyssen, for similar reasons, warns against the over-enthusiastic claiming of modernism for feminism: 'The wholesale theorization of modernist writing as feminine simply ignores the powerful masculinist and misogynist current within the trajectory of modernism.'[31]

In the visual arts it is also possible to identify the central themes of modernism. According to Griselda Pollock, masculine sexuality and in particular its commercial exchange dominate the works seen as the 'founding monuments of modern art'.[32] (Manet's *A Bar at the Folies-Bergère* and *Olympia*, Picasso's *Demoiselles d'Avignon* are examples of an extensive genre.) This is related to the contemporary types of representation of space – the street, the bar, the café. The spaces painted by women, denied equal access to the public sphere with men, were primarily domestic spaces. Again, we could pursue this analysis to try to explain the absence of women from the modernist canon, whose primary subject-matter was off limits to them.

But, as this reference to public and private spaces already indicates, we cannot understand gender differentiation around content without relating this back to the social differences in which it occurs. For the issue here is men's and women's very different experiences of 'the modern'. That is not to say that modernism is straightforwardly the art of modernity. Modernism is a particular set of practices and ideologies of representation; modernity is a specific historical experience.[33] Modernism dates from the late nineteenth century; modernity is variously placed at the same date, identified as a sixteenth-century phenomenon, or located somewhere between the two. Baudelaire, undoubtedly the poet of modernity since he writes of the experience of the modern age and the modern city, is not in any definition a 'modernist' writer in aesthetic terms. And yet there is a relationship between the two. Raymond Williams has argued that there are 'decisive links between the practices and ideas of the avant-garde movements of the twentieth century and the specific conditions and relationships of the twentieth-century metropolis'.[34] The city experience, with its antecedents in the nineteenth century, is characterized by alienation and isolation among a crowd of strangers, and by the presence of crime and danger, as well as by the more positive vitality and 'possibilities of unity' offered by the very diversity of city life.[35] Modernism itself developed in these circumstances, though

Williams is careful not to identify it with the experience of modernity. 'It is not the general themes of response to the city and its modernity which compose anything that can be properly called Modernism. It is rather the new and specific location of the artists and intellectuals of this movement within the changing cultural milieu of the metropolis.'[36] In other words, describing modernity in art or literature does not constitute modernism. But, as Williams goes on to suggest, the radical transformations *in* the arts were made possible first by the changing social relations and cultural institutions, and second by the dislocations in language effected by immigration and the consequently frequent need for a second language. In such a way it becomes possible to see the relationship between the experience of modernity, its articulation in culture, and the formal innovations in artistic language which constitute modernism.

If modernism is, in this sense, the art of modernity, women's absence from the canon becomes a little clearer, for the subject matter embraced by the new cultural forms is primarily a masculine one. The experience of anonymity in the city, the fleeting, impersonal contacts described by social commentators like Georg Simmel[37], the possibility of unmolested strolling and observation first seen by Baudelaire, and then analysed by Walter Benjamin[38] were entirely the experiences of men. By the late nineteenth century, middle-class women had been more or less consigned (in ideology if not always in reality) to the private sphere. The public world of work, city life, bars, and cafés was barred to the respectable woman.[39] (As Rachel Bowlby shows, by the end of the nineteenth century shopping was an important activity for women, the rise of the department store and of the consumer society providing a highly legitimate, if limited, participation in the public.[40] But, of course, the literature of modernity and the themes of modernism were not concerned with shopping, and women remained invisible in the continuing preoccupation with the 'real' concerns of modern life. Similarly, the experience of working-class women in that period, excluded by economic necessity from the ideological injunction to domesticity, and continuing to pass through the streets on their way to work, is no part of the new culture.)

Three things are clear. First, the definition of the modern, and the nature of modernism, derived from the experience of men and hence excluded women. Second, women, of course, had their own experience of the modern world, and were engaged in articulating this in literature and painting. And third, there is no doubt that women writers and artists were as much involved in the revolution in literary and visual languages as men. That is why it is both possible and essential to rewrite the history of modernism, showing women's role in it. This means that we need to look again at the classics of modernism, to discover what we can now see as their very particular perspective on 'the modern'. It is not that men did not depict women. But the masculine definition of modernity produced a skewed account, in which the only women visible (apart from at home in the family) were 'marginal' women or women involved in less than respectable occupations. I have already referred to the extensive genre of bar and brothel scenes, discussed by Griselda Pollock. And although it is always risky to select particular works to illustrate a point, it is instructive to compare paintings of the city by men and by women in the period of early modernism. Kirchner's *Strasse mit roter Kokotte* of 1914–25 (Plate 3) shows the street as the province of the prostitute. George Grosz's 1915 *Café* (Plate 4) has a similar, though more viciously executed, theme. August Macke's *Hutladen* (Hatshop) of 1913 (Plate 5) depicts woman in her respectable public role of window-shopping (though since her back is turned this is hardly an investigation of female experience).

How could women portray the public, given their exclusion from most of its institutions and practices? Gwen John provides one possible answer. In *Corner of the Artist's Room in Paris*, 1907–10 (Plate 6), the interior is made to stand for the exterior, the artist's parasol and jacket referring to her recent excursion into the male domain, the window and blurred outline of a building indicating the city she has chosen as her home but in which she cannot feel at ease. In literature and in painting we are familiar with work by women that abandons the public world and shows the domestic environment. But women's particular access to the public, and even their exclusion from it, can also be portrayed in oblique ways, as in Gwen John's painting.

Griselda Pollock has suggested that women artists may deploy space in their work in a way which is consonant with their gender-differentiated experience of the world. Looking at French Impressionist painters, and in particular Berthe Morisot and Mary Cassatt, she notes the frequent theme of the balcony, veranda, or embankment in their work, and argues that the balcony (as, for example, in Mary Cassatt's 1883 *Susan on the Balcony Holding a Dog* (Plate 7) demarcates 'the boundary . . . between the spaces of masculinity and femininity inscribed at the level of both what spaces are open to men and women and what relation a man or woman has to that space and its occupants'.[41] The juxtaposition of two spatial systems in the canvas is peculiar to women's paintings, while similar works by men allow apparently free access to the world beyond the window or the balcony.

It is thus possible to undertake the analysis of work by women which does represent or allude to 'the public', and thereby both to understand women's particular relationship to that sphere, and to begin to expand our notion of 'modern life' to include the female experience of it. In literature we can reread those stories in which women write about the excursion into the public, or the view of the public from the domestic sphere. Virginia Woolf's short story *Mrs Dalloway in Bond Street*, written in 1922/3, is not only a story about shopping for gloves; it is at the same time an account of a middle-class woman walking through London, observing (and being observed by) others, talking to a male acquaintance she meets, and reflecting on change since the pre-war days.[42] Here modernist strategies (breaking the narrative flow, shifting from the objective to the subjective, following the haphazard movement of the character's mind, switching briefly to the point of view of another person, and so on) facilitate this novel female account. Mrs Dalloway's perceptions, her thoughts, her selective view of what surrounds her are those of a woman, of her age and class, and produce a female account of the modern city. The fat lady in the motor car has 'taken every sort of trouble', but shocks Mrs Dalloway by wearing diamonds and orchids in the morning. Lady Bexborough in her carriage, with a white glove loose at her wrist, looks shabby to her. She notes the motherliness and homeliness of Victoria's statue, and reflects on the present Queen's duties of visiting hospitals and opening bazaars. Walking through Westminster and past the Palace evokes no thoughts about politics or war, except for the memory of the bereaved mother met at last night's party. This is not to stress the superficiality of women's thoughts, or their tendency to export the private into the public, but rather to comment on the ways in which women's perspective transforms the spaces of masculinity.

For the most part, however, women writers and artists did specialize in depicting the domestic sphere, portraying the world they knew best, and to which they had unlimited access. Griselda Pollock argues that here too modernism allowed women to produce new images which dislocated the dominant ideas of femininity and of women's proper role. For example, where men paint women at their toilet or bath in the voyeuristic mode characteristic of Degas or Manet, women paint the same theme with woman as subject rather than body.[43] More interestingly, formal dislocation can stand for social or personal unease. (Pollock considers Mary Cassatt's 1878 *Girl in a Blue Armchair*, in which a young girl, sprawled in a large chair, is seen from an unusually low angle, evoking, according to Pollock, the child's sense of space of the room.[44])

Now it is also conceivable that male writers and painters can, sometimes unintentionally, portray women's unease in patriarchal culture, including in their prescribed domestic role. Eunice Lipton has analysed Degas's 'uneasy images of women and modern life'.[45] We could see Vuillard's *Girl in an Interior* (1910; Plate 8) as a representation of a young woman hemmed in and trapped by the domestic (the tea things laid, the enclosure of space in which she sits, and so on). We could discuss Joyce's or Henry James's insights into women's experience in the modern world. We might want to say there are limitations on men's understanding of this, or we may praise their ability to see from women's point of view. But the central point is that the literature and art of modernism, as currently defined and categorized, marginalizes or excludes women's experience, gives priority to the public world (with a substantial genre of work showing men's perspective on the private). And it is now possible to question this categorization, and to show how many women artists, experimenting in aesthetic form, were formulating the specifically female experience of modernity. The new literary and visual forms and strategies were invented and deployed to capture and represent the changed situation of women in the modern world, both in the private and in the public arenas.

The fact that women are absent from the modernist canon, therefore, is cause for critically examining that canon rather than for reluctantly accepting that modernism proved inaccessible to women. Its foregrounding of specific key themes and subjects (the war, the public sphere, masculine sexuality, and so on) is not in any way essential to modernism as aesthetic strategy, as the participation of women from Impressionism to Abstract Expressionism testifies. We come back, then, to the question of whether modernism, with its deconstructive, questioning strategies, is particularly well suited to a feminist art practice – whether the new 'feminine sentence' identified by Virginia Woolf is capable, in a way earlier forms of writing were not, of expressing alternatives to patriarchal culture.

There can be no unqualified positive, or for that matter negative, answer to this question. Feminist critics are right to identify the political potential in modernist strategies, and if we look back at the characteristics listed by Eugene Lunn (self-reflexiveness, montage, paradox, 'dehumanisation'), it is clear that such destabilizing strategies have the ability to disrupt and interrogate the prevailing modes of viewing and reading, and hence to expose the ideological character of representation, and put into question what has hitherto been taken for granted. This is as true for feminist practice as it is for any other radical cultural politics. Moreover, those strategies first developed in the 1920s are by no means outmoded, as many people have assumed. It is true that modernism as institution has been absorbed into the academy, its politics neutralized, and its techniques denuded of their shock value by their very familiarity in popular culture. But the judicious use of montage, defamiliariza- tion, and other modernist tactics can still achieve that dislocation of thought aimed at by the early political modernists. Two feminist exhibitions in the 1980s have confirmed this: *Beyond the Purloined Image*, curated by Mary Kelly and shown at the Riverside Studios in London in 1983; and *Difference: On Representation and Sexuality*, shown in New York in 1984 and in London in 1985.[46]

Psychoanalytic and semiotic theories also demonstrate that aesthetic strategies that subvert the rule of logic, reason, and realism can release the repressed voice of those who are silenced. Thus Kristeva's analysis of the 'semiotic' character of avant-garde writing has proved extremely suggestive for feminists. Other French feminists, encouraging a writing which comes 'from the body', also speak of the possibility of women's voice finding its expression in the free play of modernist language.[47] Although any lingering essentialism in this account must be firmly resisted, the recognition that entry into language and entry into patriarchal culture are closely connected (though not identical, as some have argued) points to the liberatory potential of a writing or an art which comes from the unconscious (or, in Kristeva's terms, from the semiotic chora[48]).

But there are also some reservations to be made. In the first place, modernism as *institution* had clearly lost its radical potential by the middle of this century.[49] We have also seen how the institutions of modernism (criticism, art history, galleries, publishers) excluded women from their construction of a modernist canon. Nor can we assume that the specific modernist strategies identified by Lunn and others are intrinsically progressive. As Franco Moretti has argued, the politics of irony and ambiguity are by now equally part of the hegemonic culture. 'There is a complicity between modernist irony and indifference to history'.[50] And, as is well known, we are not short of examples of modernist artists and writers whose political affiliations were with the right or even with fascism.

What we can still insist on, however, is the radical potential of the deconstructive strategies of modernist culture, when founded in an appropriate political and historical analysis. It is in this sense that we may still confidently look forward to the continuing production of modernist work by feminists. In conjunction with the overdue rewriting of the history of modernism, this will ensure that the exciting complementarity of feminist politics and modernist aesthetics is not abandoned because of intimidation in the face of the canon-makers.

NOTES

1   Virginia Woolf, 'Mr Bennett and Mrs Brown', in *Collected Essays*, vol. 1 (London, Hogarth Press, 1966), p. 320.
2   Alice Jardine, 'Opaque Texts and Transparent Contexts: The Political Difference of Julia Kristeva', in Nancy K. Miller (ed.), *The Poetics of Gender* (New York: Columbia University Press, 1986), p. 105.
3   Woolf, 'Mr Bennett and Mrs Brown', p. 334.
4   Ibid., p. 331.
5   Ibid., p. 320.
6   Virginia Woolf, 'Women and Fiction', in Michèle Barrett (ed.), *Virginia Woolf: Women and Writing* (London, The Women's Press, 1979), p. 48.
7   Virginia Woolf, 'Dorothy Richardson', in Barrett (ed.), *Virginia Woolf: Women and Writing*, p. 191.
8   Sandra M. Gilbert and Susan Gubar, *No Man's Land. The Place of the Woman Writer in the Twentieth Century*, vol. 1: *The War of the Words* (New Haven, Conn., and London, Yale University Press, 1988), p. xii.
9   Jardine, 'Opaque Texts and Transparent Contexts'. Also her *Gynesis, Configurations of Woman and Modernity* (Ithaca and London, Cornell University Press, 1985).
10 Julia Kristeva, *Revolution in Poetic Language* (New York, Columbia University Press, 1984).

11   Mary Kelly, 'Re-viewing Modernist Criticism', *Screen*, 22, 3 (1981); Griselda Pollock, 'Screening the Seventies: Sexuality and Representation in Feminist Practice – A Brechtian Perspective', in her *Vision and Difference: Femininity, Feminism and Histories of Art* (London, Routledge, 1988).
12   Perry Anderson, 'Modernity and Revolution', *New Left Review*, 144 (March/April 1984), pp. 103, 113.
13   Ibid., pp. 102–3, 112.
14   For example, Malcolm Bradbury and James McFarlane (eds), *Modernism 1890–1930* (Harmondsworth, Penguin, 1976); H. Stuart Hughes, *Consciousness and Society: The Reorientation of European Social Thought 1890–1930*, (1959; St Albans, Paladin, 1974).
15   For example, Shari Benstock, *Women of the Left Bank: Paris 1900–40* (London, Virago Press, 1987); Gillian Hanscombe and Virginia L. Smyers, *Writing for their Lives: The Modernist Women 1910–40* (London, The Women's Press, 1987). Eugene Lunn, in *Marxism and Modernism: An Historical Study of Lukács, Brecht, Benjamin, and Adorno* (London, Verso, 1985), decides to focus on 'the period 1920–50, and especially 1928–40' (p. 4).
16   Marshall Berman, *All That is Solid Melts into Air: The Experience of Modernity* (London, Verso, 1983); T. J. Clark, *The Painting of Modern Life: Paris in the Art of Manet and his Followers* (London, Thames and Hudson, 1984).
17   Lunn, *Marxism and Modernism* p. 34.
18   Ibid., p. 34–7.
19   Hughes, *Consciousness and Society*.
20   Alan Bullock, 'The Double Image', in Bradbury and McFarlane (eds), *Modernism*, pp. 62–7.
21   Frederick J. Hoffman, *The Twenties: American Writing in the Postwar Decade* (New York, Collier, 1962). Cited by Benstock, *Women of the Left Bank*, p. 26.
22   Ibid., p. 19.
23   Hanscombe and Smyers, *Writing for their Lives*.
24   For example, Eleanor Tufts, *Our Hidden Heritage: Five Centuries of Women Artists* (London, Paddington Press, 1974); Karen Petersen and J. J. Wilson, *Women Artists: Recognition and Reappraisal from the Early Middle Ages to the Twentieth Century* (New York, Harper & Row, 1976); Germaine Greer, *The Obstacle Race: The Fortunes of Women Painters and their Work* (London, Secker & Warburg, 1979).
25   See Rosemary Betterton, 'How do Women Look? The Female Nude in the World of Suzanne Valadon', in R. Betterton (ed.), *Looking On: Images of Femininity in the Visual Arts and Media* (London, Pandora, 1987); Griselda Pollock, *Mary Cassatt* (London, Jupiter Books, 1980).

26 Whitney Chadwick, *Women Artists and the Surrealist Movement* (Boston, Little, Brown & Co., 1985). Note, too, the recent publication of Leonora Carrington's stories: *The House of Fear: Notes from Down Below* (New York, E.P. Dutton, 1988).

27 For example in recent exhibitions of Lee Krasner's work. *Lee Krasner Collages*, exhibition catalogue (New York, Robert Miller Gallery, 1986).

28 Griselda Pollock, 'Feminism and Modernism', in Rozsika Parker and Griselda Pollock (eds), *Framing Feminism: Art and the Women's Movement 1970–1985* (London, Pandora, 1987), pp. 86, 105.

29 Andreas Huyssen, 'Mass Culture as Woman: Modernism's Other', in *After the Great Divide: Modernism, Mass Culture and Postmodernism* (London, Macmillan, 1988).

30 Benstock, *Women of the Left Bank*, p. 26.

31 Huyssen, 'Mass Culture as Woman', p. 49.

32 Griselda Pollock, 'Modernity and Spaces of Femininity', in Pollock, *Vision and Difference*, p. 54.

33 Anderson ('Modernity and Revolution') clarifies the differences and relationship between these terms, as well as the third term, 'modernization'.

34 Raymond Williams, 'The Metropolis and the Emergence of Modernism', in Edward Timms and David Kelley (eds), *Unreal City: Urban Experience In Modern European Literature and Art* (Manchester, Manchester University Press, 1985), p. 13.

35 Ibid., pp. 15–19.

36 Ibid., p. 20.

37 George Simmel, 'The Metropolis and Mental Life', in Kurt H. Wolff (ed.), *The Sociology of George Simmel* (New York, Free Press, 1950).

38 Charles Baudelaire, 'The Painter of Modern Life', in *The Painter of Modern Life and Other Essays*, tr. and ed. Jonathan Mayne (1863; Oxford, Phaidon Press, 1964). Walter Benjamin, *Charles Baudelaire: A Lyric Poet in the Era of High Capitalism* (London, New Left Books, 1973).

39 See 'The Culture of Separate Spheres: The Role of Culture in Nineteenth-Century Public and Private Life' and 'The Invisible *Flâneuse*: Women and the Literature of Modernity', both included in this collection.

40 Rachel Bowlby, *Just Looking: Consumer Culture in Dreiser, Gissing and Zola* (London, Methuen, 1985).

41 Pollock, 'Modernity and the Spaces of Femininity', p. 62.

42 Virginia Woolf, 'Mrs Dalloway in Bond Street', in *The Complete Shorter Fiction* (London, Triad Grafton, 1987).

43 Pollock, 'Modernity and the Spaces of Femininity', pp. 80–1.

44 Ibid., p. 65. However, the problems of a feminist reading of this painting were made clear to me when I showed it in a lecture, and met

the suggestion that the low-angle view of the young girl, sprawled in the chair with her legs apart, could equally lend itself to a pornographic reading.

45 Eunice Lipton, *Looking into Degas: Uneasy Images of Women and Modern Life* (Berkeley, University of California Press, 1986).

46 As Griselda Pollock has argued, Brecht is still of great relevance to feminists in the 1980s ('Screening the Seventies').

47 For a discussion of this, see 'Women's Knowledge and Women's Art', included in this collection.

48 Kristeva, *Revolution in Poetic Language*, pp. 40, 82–5.

49 See Suzi Gablik, *Has Modernism Failed?* (London, Thames and Hudson, 1984).

50 Franco Moretti, 'The Spell of Indecision', in C. Nelson and L. Grossberg (eds), *Marxism and the Interpretation of Culture* (London, Macmillan, 1988), p. 343.

5

Women's Knowledge and
Women's Art

Can there be such a thing as 'women's writing'? More specifically, in a patriarchal culture, in which institution, language, and regimes of representation collude in the marginalization of women's experience and in the silencing of women's voice, is it possible for women to articulate the suppressed by new aesthetic strategies? Those feminists who propose the notion of *l'écriture féminine* argue that it is. This view has also had supporters in other traditions than contemporary French feminism. Virginia Woolf suggested that there is such a thing as a 'woman's sentence',[1] to be found in the work of women modernists like Dorothy Richardson.[2]

The idea that literary forms can be radically altered in order to accommodate and express women's experience is now well established in some areas of feminist criticism. 'Feminine writing' is rediscovered in the work of past authors, and created in contemporary experimental texts, influenced by Hélène Cixous's concept of 'writing from the body'[3] and by the work of other French feminist novelists and critics. Important in this development has been Julia Kristeva's analysis of what she has called 'the revolution in poetic language', in which she claims that certain avant-garde texts from the late nineteenth century explored the possibility of subverting the patriarchal order in representation by writing from the 'semiotic chora' – the pre-Oedipal (and therefore, in Lacanian terms, the pre-Symbolic) moment.[4] The fact that the writers Kristeva discusses are men (Mallarmé and Lautréamont) is not the point, since what she is trying to do is to examine the origins, in modernist literature, of a type of writing which escapes the confines of the predominating patriarchal culture. Such writing would clearly be available for a feminist cultural politics.

The concept of 'feminine writing' has also been extended to the visual arts. Nancy Spero's work has recently been discussed as an example of *la peinture féminine*.[5] The idea that women can write, paint, and produce culture which is no longer constrained within forms alien to their experience has proved an attractive and a liberating one for many artists and critics. In this essay, I want to consider some of the more problematic issues raised by this work and this politics, in particular looking more closely at what is meant by 'women's art'. To the extent that this concept depends on certain ideas of 'women's knowledge' (that is, the assumption that women's and men's experience and knowledge is in some important sense *different*), it seems essential to discuss questions of aesthetics in relation to questions of epistemology. I shall therefore be looking at recent work on women and science and women and philosophy, in order to explore further the key concept of 'women's knowledge'.

The fact that the possibility of 'women's voice' in culture has been raised at all is in many ways the culmination of fifteen or more years of feminist work in literary and art criticism. This work has systematically demonstrated the comprehensively patriarchal nature of culture – its institutions and ideologies of production and reception, its regimes of representation, and its formal and textual characteristics. First, feminists have addressed the question of why the history of art is almost entirely a history of men's work. (The same question can be asked of the history of music, the history of architecture, and of most other cultural forms. Even in the case of literature, where there have always been published women novelists, an examination of the processes of cultural production reveals an abundance of discriminatory practices which operate against women.) More recently, feminist art historians have turned from the earlier project of rediscovering 'lost' women artists, republishing 'lost' women authors (through feminist presses), and of rewriting the histories of art and literature. Instead, they have insisted on the importance of examining and exposing the structural and ideological obstacles to women's success in the arts, both in the past and in the contemporary present.

Secondly, there has been a great of deal of work on gender and representation, which has analysed the ways in which women have been depicted in literature and painting. This is not simply a question of exposing a narrow range of stereotypes, but more a recognition of the way in which the very category of 'woman' is constructed in representation. What becomes clear is the formal and conventional impossibility of a feminist heroine, of an ideologically subversive plot, or of a female body perceived without all the connotations and meanings of a patriarchal system of representation and of viewing.

Lastly, theories of reception have been mobilized to expose the denial to women of a subject position as reader. Jonathan Culler asks what it would be like to read the opening of Thomas Hardy's *The Mayor of Casterbridge* (which deals with a wife-sale) as a woman.[6] Just as art criticism and film criticism have demonstrated the ways in which texts constitute their readers/viewers as male, so feminist literary critics have identified that necessary process which has been called the 'immasculation of the reader' – that is, the need for women, if they are to be competent readers in our culture, to take on the point of view of men.[7]

In the face of this relentless exclusion of women from culture, feminists raise the question of what a *different* culture would be like. What is the possibility for women to write (or paint) from their own experience, no longer mediated by the culture and point of view of men? And where, if anywhere, are the spaces the dominant culture allows for this expression? The literary critic, Elaine Showalter, has proposed that the primary task of feminist criticism is the identification of the key characteristics of women's writing – an exercise which she calls *gynocritics*. This will deal with the 'history, styles, themes, genres, and structures of writing by women'.[8] To explore the basis of women's writing, Showalter employs the concept of the 'wild zone', borrowed from the anthropologist, Edwin Ardener. Ardener describes the way in which, in many cultures, areas of women's lives and experience are marginalized by the dominant culture. Where the experiences and perspectives of men and women overlap, then the dominant culture and language will be adequate to describe them. But since cultures are all patriarchal, those areas of experience which are specific to women are excluded, and cannot be articulated or shared within the available discourse.[9] This is the 'wild zone'.

In 1986 there was a report about the discovery of a secret script, apparently still in use in China and dating from the Chang dynasty (1600 to 1100 BC).[10] The script, which used an inverted system of grammar and syntax very different from Chinese, and was written with ink and brush and without punctuation, was said to have been used only by women, uniting them in 'an exclusive sisterhood'. This kind of anthropological evidence suggests the possibility for women of articulating the 'wild zone' of their own experience, outside the dominant culture and language of men.

Nevertheless, the notion of a 'wild zone', and the idea that we can somehow develop language outside culture, is problematic. As Showalter says, there is no way in which we can talk about the 'wild zone', the muted voice, the new language, outside the dominant structure.[11] We could add that there is no way in which those who are marginalized by the dominant culture can develop alternative cultural forms other than from their basis in that culture, for this is where they learn to speak, where they are socialized, and where they enter culture as gendered subjects with the ability to communicate. (Similar arguments have been made against Kristeva's suggestion that avant-garde writing emerges from the semiotic chora, for here too it must be stressed that *any* communication presupposes entry into the Symbolic.) Showalter concludes that women's writing is more a double-edged discourse than something entirely separate. It embodies the social, cultural, and literary heritage of both the muted and the dominant groups.

We need to look a little more closely at the assumption that women *are* excluded from culture, if this is to be more than a polemical claim. That is, we need to know what is meant by claiming that culture and knowledge are 'male'. We also need to be more specific about the argument that women are silenced by or excluded from the dominant culture. What are the mechanisms and practices through which this occurs? Lastly, we can then come back to the question of how it is possible for women to articulate their experience in language, in writing, and in art.

The institutional organization of knowledge operates to marginalize women, as well as to reinforce the gender inequalities in contemporary society. The historical development of the different disciplines, arbitrary as it has been from the point of view of our actual experience in the world and in everyday life, reinforces the division of the sexes. We have come to study economics in isolation from history and from politics. We study philosophy in a way which detaches ideas from their origins and meanings in the social and material world. We study art and literature as totally separate from the political and social circumstances in which they are produced and consumed. This historical segregation of areas of investigation has other kinds of implication for knowledge, criticism, and power relations, apart from questions raised by feminism. But from the point of view of gender inequalities, it is clear that it is more or less impossible to address these issues within the framework of the mainstream academic tradition. To make any sense of the question of why there have been so few successful women artists we need to look at extra-aesthetic processes – the social, ideological, and economic situation of women, the institutions and practices of the arts in a particular period in terms of their social, financial, material organization, and so on. The question of why women are 'hidden from history' is not just a question about the discipline of history, though to answer it we will have to examine that discipline and its own specific kinds of formulation and exclusion. It is also a question about the *wider* context of historical events, which traditional historical method cannot perceive.

In short, a sociological perspective is essential in each of the disciplines, to make clear the circumstances which produce certain limited types of knowledge and certain particular gender imbalances. But even within the discipline of sociology itself these artificial divisions are visible. The sociology of industry, the sociology of politics, the sociology of education, and most of the other sub-areas within the discipline may be prepared to look at gender these days, observing women's disadvantaged position in each domain. But only an *integrated* sociological account could explain this, for women's position in the labour market (and, we could add, women's place in cultural production) is inextricably linked with two other things: the history of gender divisions and of the institutions in question, and the contemporary situation of men and women in the domestic sphere. Alongside the other areas of sociological study, the sociology of the family has a fairly long pedigree. But this approach to the domestic sphere as something separate merely compounds the separation of work and home, of public and private. It is only with the relatively recent rise of feminist sociology that it has become possible to *relate* the two areas rather than treating them as completely distinct.

The institutional organization of knowledge thus mirrors and produces the gender biases of the social world. The public is separated from the private in the dominant conceptualization, and because women have historically always been secondary in, or marginal to, the public sphere, they are similarly constructed as secondary in knowledge. Either they are totally invisible (as in the sociology of industry until recently), or at best secondary (filling less important roles);[12] or their own sphere of operation is completely ignored and absent from the literature. In fact, as feminist historians have pointed out,[13] it has never been correct to argue that from the nineteenth century men occupied the public sphere and women the private sphere. The interconnections are complex, and each sex has its own particular access to and involvement in both spheres. But only an intellectual approach which incorporates and explores the historical development of the public and the private and the relationship between them will be able to comprehend the real social relations of gender.

The fact that institutionalized knowledge reflects (and also produces) gender inequalities, giving priority to men's areas of knowledge and of social life, is connected to the development of the professions since the nineteenth century. The separation of new and distinct disciplines out of earlier more general areas of knowledge was itself the product of the increasing professionalization of work, including, in this case, of academic work. This coincided with the period in which the separation of spheres took on its most exaggerated form in western societies, as the centralization of production in larger units, outside the home, produced the physical conditions for this increasingly fragmented and compartmentalized way of life. This development was compounded by the growth of bureaucracies (another form of non-domestic, centralized work), and by processes of urbanization, notably the expansion of middle-class suburbs, which reinforced the separation of work and home. Feminist historians have documented this process, and also identified the role of the specific ideology of gender, domesticity, and male and female roles which accompanied and facilitated it.

The implications of this for the institutionalization of knowledge were twofold. In the first place, women were excluded from the production of knowledge, which was predominantly redefined as academic and professional thought. As with all the other professions, whether they were new areas of work (like engineering and banking) or traditional areas, newly defined (and narrowed) as professions (such as medicine and education), the academy was a male preserve. Second, the subject-matter of the new disciplines was bound to reflect the interests of its practitioners – namely men. Thus, those areas of experience and knowledge which were specifically women's systematically failed to be represented in the 'knowledge' produced in the academy and in the institutions of intellectual life. The knowledge-producers were dealing with what they knew best, and they were also operating with the existing hierarchy of importance, in which the public (predominantly the male sphere) took precedence over the private (associated with women, and perceived as the female sphere). At the same time, women's 'public' existence (in factories, in offices, in the street and in the department store) was ignored.

This issue can be related directly to the earlier discussion of women's exclusion from cultural production. For in this area too, the institutions (the Academies, the art schools, the journals, and so on) were run by men, and the ideologies of creativity were entirely male-defined. And those processes which in one way or another go back centuries, culminating in a particular division of labour after the Industrial Revolution, can be followed through to the present day. The ideology of domesticity and of women's role may be much transformed since the Victorian period, and women may have entered the labour market in large numbers. Nowadays they are not banned from Academy membership or barred from the life-class. Nevertheless, any look at major national and international exhibitions confirms that men predominate in the visual arts. Women's work, across the arts, is given considerably less space in critical discussion. And the literary and art historical establishments for the most part remain very resistant to feminist work and to the necessary reconceptualization of the history and practice of the arts.

So far I have discussed various institutional obstacles to the equal expression of men's and women's experience, and I have suggested that both the development of the disciplines and the rise of the professions have tended to produce a knowledge that is partial and 'male'. Research on language has also suggested that a patriarchal culture silences women through the very concepts and linguistic practices which prevail. Descriptive linguistics has shown that women are often described relationally ('a man and his wife', for example), and that those supposedly generic terms 'man' and 'he' (as in 'a problem for the scientist in the twentieth century is that he . . .') *don't* in fact operate as neutral in respect to gender. Dale Spender demonstrates this with the telling comparison of the perfectly acceptable 'man is the only primate that commits rape' and the totally ridiculous statement 'man, unlike other mammals, has difficulties in giving birth'.[14] Vocabulary is also biased in terms of non-equivalents: for example, the very different connotations of 'master' and 'mistress' expose a whole history of meanings and of sexual inequalities. Descriptive linguistics also claims to have perceived significant differences in language use between men and women. Women are said to use 'tag questions' more often than men ('isn't it?', 'didn't they?'), registering a tentativeness far less common among male speakers. Men are said to speak more than women in a mixed forum, and to interrupt far more often. Contributions by women to a discussion are more likely to be ignored, while points made by men will be taken up by other speakers. Although some of the more simplistic of these claims about sexism in language have been contested, including by more sophisticated feminist studies and analyses,[15] there is no doubt that linguistic practices and language itself construct women and men differentially, subordinating women and obstructing their equal participation in discourse and, hence, social life.

Kristeva's analysis of avant-garde writing, mentioned earlier, is the basis for a different kind of argument about the patriarchal nature of language (and also, as I indicated, for the possibility of a new, non-patriarchal speech). Starting from the Lacanian premise that for the child entry into language, into the Symbolic, is at the same time entry into patriarchy, Kristeva suggests that certain kinds of writing have been able to evade the apparently monolithic control of the Symbolic. Those texts which are produced from the rhythms and pulsions of the semiotic chora – the pre-linguistic, pre-Oedipal experience – and which are in this sense antecedent to representation, offer the possibility of a non-patriarchal expression. I have already referred to the difficulties with this argument. First, in that the writers Kristeva discusses are both male, there is nothing inherently 'feminine' about the use of the 'semiotic rhythm within language'.[16] Second, as Kristeva herself recognizes, in practice such a possibility only exists *within* the Symbolic.[17] Even the identification of patriarchy with entry into the Symbolic has been questioned, since the acquisition of language precedes the Oedipal phase in the child's development. But what is important about this feminist application of Lacanian theory is the acknowledgement of the crucial link between language and patriarchy, and of the linguistic constitution of the patriarchal regime.

A third area of gender bias in knowledge, after the institutional and the linguistic, is the methodological. Here I shall talk mainly about the social sciences, though it can equally be shown that research methods, systems of classification, conceptual frameworks, and theoretical models are partial and distorted in exactly the same way in other disciplines. The collection of statistics themselves has been shown to be biased.[18] For example social surveys on education, or social mobility, or poverty, generally take the family as the unit of analysis, and begin from the 'head of household', usually the male head. Mobility studies notoriously trace sons of fathers. Not only does this research totally ignore what women do. It also obscures important intra-familial differences, which might well illuminate the material. (For example, where working-class men are married to middle-class women, educational success or longer-term upward mobility on the part of the child might be better explained.) There are, of course, real problems in taking smaller units of analysis (looking solely at individuals might hide the important dynamics of family power relations). But the fact is that mainstream social science operates with the uncritical categories of everyday life, which are biased in respect of gender.

Some feminist sociologists have claimed that even the sacred dogma of 'objectivity' is a sexist notion. Ann Oakley, for example, argues that the accepted orthodoxy on methods of interviewing is inappropriate for female social scientists interviewing other women.[19] The idea of the detached, impartial, controlling interviewer, whose own views and values are kept out of the dialogue, is one which is unacceptable for feminist research. Moreover, we could add, it is one which will fail to get at any real experience. Particularly in her work with mothers, Oakley found the ideal of distance and non-involvement was impossible to achieve, as well as undesirable to attempt. The hierarchical relationship it sets up and the manipulation of the subject were replaced by a co-operative, two-way relationship, in which her own experience and identity came into play in developing a connection which elicited the understanding she was looking for in her research.

It should be stressed that this does not mean either that only feminists should reject simplistic notions of objectivity and detachment (the implication is that *any* research will be better if it is based on dialogue); or that we must henceforth associate quantitative work with men and qualitative work with women. The latter is an assumption sometimes made. It is as well to bear in mind David Morgan's reminder that qualitative sociology has often consisted of brave males venturing out into areas of danger. 'Qualitative methodology and ethnography after all has its own brand of *machismo* with its image of the male sociologist bringing back news from the fringes of society, the lower depths, the mean streets, areas traditionally 'off limits' to women investigators.'[20] As I will argue in relation to feminist epistemology, however, an important part of the argument about method has to do with the congruence of officially prescribed techniques with male experience in our culture, and the associated incompatibility of these methods with women's lives and ways of communicating. Dorothy Smith has argued that sociology is also based on a kind of 'conceptual imperialism'.[21] In our culture women are assigned to the home (in ideology, if not necessarily always in practice). Men, on the other hand, are assigned to the world of work, and the abstract conceptual mode of knowledge that goes with this. Women's role is to mediate for men the relationship between the conceptual mode and the concrete forms in which is it realized. She argues for a woman-centred perspective, which will substitute for abstract concepts a new kind of knowledge, grounded in experience and doing justice to the complexity of human existence, not just the segregated and distorted perspective of men. In the rest of this essay I shall look at recent work in feminist epistemology which helps us to explore such questions and to examine the alleged male bias in knowledge and science.

The following is the starting point of a collection of feminist essays on epistemology, methodology, and science:

> What counts as knowledge must be grounded on experience. Human experience differs according to the kinds of activities and social relations in which humans engage. Women's experience systematically differs from the male experience upon which knowledge claims have been grounded. Thus the experience on which the prevailing claims to social and natural knowledge are founded is, first of all, only partial human experience only partially understood: namely, masculine experience as understood by men.[22]

By now it is no heresy to suggest that the acquisition of knowledge in the scientific process is a haphazard, accidental affair. Philosophers of science and sociologists of science have demonstrated the very *un*-scientific way in which hypotheses are formed, experiments devised, data gathered, and results written up. The direction of science itself is determined by the extra-scientific considerations of government policy and of the needs and preferences of funding agencies. The transformation of social science in Britain during the 1980s, increasingly in a direction of policy-oriented research, and at the expense of the survival of theoretically and critically inclined university departments, is a clear example of this process. It is useful, I think, to see the feminist intervention into the philosophy of science and knowledge as part of the critique of earlier naïve notions of science (social as well as natural science) as the pursuit of Truth, discovered in accordance with strict rules of Objectivity and Impartiality. Scientific knowledge, like any other kind of knowledge, is systematically related to human values and interests, and is necessarily a product of the limited and partial perspective of its practitioners. Inasmuch, therefore, as science is dominated by men, the scientific process is bound to produce a body of knowledge reflecting the lives and interests of men.

Hilary Rose, a sociologist of science, stresses the urgency of the feminist critique. In her view, 'the attitudes dominant within science and technology must be transformed, for their telos is nuclear annihilation'.[23] Her argument is that the destructive direction taken by science is a result of the fact that it is a very partial knowledge, produced by men and founded in the false separation of 'hand, brain and heart'. This separation she traces to the division of labour in society, and the denigration of reproduction and caring labour in western culture. In her view, it is only by transcending this division of labour that we will be able to develop a new scientific knowledge and technology which will 'enable humanity to live in harmony rather than in antagonism with nature'.[24] In this we have a critical theory of knowledge which relates the androcentric nature of science to the very different social roles and tasks of men and women in society. Like Dorothy Smith, Rose is proposing an experiential account of scientific practice, though one firmly located in the social relations in which experience is gained. (This sociological commitment rescues the account from any danger of essentialism, although some of the formulations of both Smith and Rose carry hints of sympathy for that feminism which subscribes to the existence of certain innate female characteristics. Hilary Rose's concluding sentence in this essay, invoking the 'baby socks, webs of wool, photos and flowers' which peace activists at Greenham Common thread through the wire fence round the military base, is unfortunate in carrying these connotations.)

This is an explanation of the distortion of science and knowledge in patriarchal culture in terms of the social relations and social roles of men and women. The argument is that science, dominated by men, manifests that kind of alienated, abstract nature which is characteristic of work in industrialized society. 'Objectivity' is a formal ideal which is in fact merely the representation of the way in which men have increasingly been obliged to live. The suggestion is that women, on the other hand, because of their continuing participation in 'caring labour', are likely to produce knowledge which is not based on the separation of subject and object and, hence, on a misguided conception of the possibility of a detached, pure science.

The social historical account of knowledge-formation, and of the role of gender in this process, is crucial. But there is one important question which it does not answer, and that is *why* it is the case that men are confined to the abstract mode of reasoning and thought. To relate this to gender roles does not really get us any further, because we still have to explain, first, what the basis for such role differentiation is or was, and second the phenomenon of the advance of alienated labour itself. Childcare arrangements are no explanation, for as we know these vary enormously from one society to another, and from one period to another. Essentialist notions of intrinsically 'feminine' or 'masculine' work are unacceptable (since sociology and history make clear the social construction of these categories). Theories of industrialization and of the rise and development of capitalism deal with the structures and processes of contemporary industrial society (as well as its institutions and ideologies), without engaging with the alleged complicity between 'masculinity' and 'objectivity', between men and abstract thought, between patriarchy and the dominance of an ideology of neutral, disinterested science.

Recent work by feminists, particularly certain American philosophers of science, has addressed this issue in psychoanalytic terms. It is interesting that the most influential work here has been object-relations theory, and not, as is more the case in Europe, and in feminist literary and film studies, the Freudian and Lacanian branches of psychoanalytic theory. The work of Nancy Chodorow and Dorothy Dinnerstein has been particularly important here, although they have not written specifically on science and epistemology.[25] They have both argued that as a result of the Oedipal drama boys learn a greater sense of separateness and autonomy than girls. This is because, in a society in which women do the nurturing, boys have to separate clearly from the mother, in order to adopt the male identity. As Nancy Hartsock puts it 'male ego-formation necessarily requires repressing this first relation and negating the mother'.[26] For girls, on the other hand, the problem might be the *inability* to differentiate. (And indeed feminists have explained problems specific to women, such as eating disorders, in terms of this early childhood scenario, and the mother–daughter relationship. For girls, and women, the problem is often one of not having clearly enough defined ego boundaries.)

As a result of this wrench from the mother, this dramatic shift into autonomy, which breaks the pre-Oedipal attachment, males continue to repress ties to the other (because of a fear of re-incorporation and engulfment), and are unable to experience themselves relationally. To quote Nancy Hartsock again: 'Girls, because of female parenting, are less differentiated from others than boys, more continuous with and related to the external object world.'[27]

The possible implications for theories of knowledge are clear. The commitment to objectivity is nothing other than a psychic need to retain distance. Invested in this is the man's very sense of gender identity, and in this light the fear of the female, and the fear of merging, make sense of a continuing way of being in the world founded on distance and differentiation. It is for this reason that Evelyn Fox Keller makes the connection with science: 'It would seem . . . appropriate to suggest that one possible outcome of these processes is that boys may be more inclined toward excessive and girls toward inadequate delineation – growing into men who have difficulty loving and women who retreat from science.' The result, she suggests, is 'a belief system which equates objectivity with masculinity, and a set of cultural values which simultaneously elevates what is defined as scientific and what is defined as masculine'.[28]

The real value of this approach is that it allows us to combine a social-historical analysis of gender differences in the field of science with another level of understanding which exposes the psychic mechanisms of differential gender construction. With regard to science and knowledge in general, it offers an account which links the institutional fact of male dominance both with the social realities of men's and women's lives in our culture and with the psychological needs and tendencies that these produce. The scientific ideal of 'objectivity' appears now as the formal and theoretical equivalent of a deep and fundamental aspect of the male psyche in western society.

Does this mean that we can envisage a female science, which will be more comprehensive, less destructive, more appropriate to a non-alienated, relational existence? Within feminism, opinions differ about the possibility of a 'successor science'. Evelyn Fox Keller makes it clear that existing science is not to be jettisoned. Quoting with approval Mary Ellman's jibe at men, and their tendency to take refuge in science even in personal matters (Ellman says 'men always get impersonal. If you hurt their feelings they make Boyle's Law out of it'), Keller goes on to point out that we must not forget that Boyle's Law is not wrong. 'Any effective critique of science needs to take due account of the undeniable successes of science. Boyle's Law does give us a reliable description of the relation between pressure and volume in low density gases at high temperatures.' But, she continues, 'It is crucial to recognise that it is a statement about a particular set of phenomena, prescribed to meet particular interests and described in accordance with certain agreed-upon criteria of both reliability and utility.[29]

In other words, we must recognize the partial and perspectival nature of science and knowledge, without necessarily concluding that its discoveries are false or useless. Jane Flax points out that women's experience is not in itself an adequate ground for theory since it too is partial.[30]

There is a certain consensus among many feminist philosophers that the feminist critique of knowledge and science should not make the mistake of claiming to substitute a new, 'correct' knowledge. (More radical positions, however, do make this claim, arguing that masculine science is to be rejected altogether.) I think it is most useful to adopt the strategy of Sandra Harding, one of those who takes the more liberal view of the critique of knowledge. Arguing that there are 'no true stories', she recommends a feminist intervention which, in true post-modern terms, operates the destabilization of thought, recognizing at the same time 'the permanent partiality of feminist inquiry'.[31] Although there are certain difficulties with the implied relativism of this position,[32] it is the only honest and consistent one and, moreover, it is likely to be the most effective strategically.

Feminist analyses of science and knowledge-formation have shown how it makes sense to describe the dominant culture and the dominant forms of knowledge as masculine and androcentric. They are masculine with regard to the social and power relations and the institutions in which knowledge is constructed. They are masculine in terms of the conceptual and linguistic apparatuses through which they are acquired and disseminated, and in terms of the selective nature of the subject-matter of the various disciplines of science and knowledge. And they are masculine in terms of the psychological orientation which produces a particular kind of knowledge, with its insistence on distance, objectivity, and non-relational characteristics. Can we proceed from this analysis to discuss the possibility of alternative forms of knowledge, which could be called women's knowledge? Here we are on more difficult ground.

We can certainly see that women's experience has been denied and marginalized by western culture and knowledge systems. It is the case, too, that work by feminists has begun to illuminate areas in the natural and social sciences which have been ignored so far (for example, work by medical scientists and biologists on women's health issues and by sociologists on women's paid work and women's domestic role). But these are corrective exercises rather than the result of a total reorganization of the field of knowledge. It is less easy to define the notion of 'women's knowledge' positively. One of the problems with such a notion is the risk, already referred to, of adopting an essentialist position – one which implies or even states that because of their particular characteristics (biological, reproductive, or cultural) women's world-view is different from (better than) that of men. Any such account must be posed historically, with regard to women's contemporary, socially constituted characteristics. A more serious difficulty with this kind of formulation is its invariable assumption that we can talk of the category of 'woman' or 'women'. As Sandra Harding points out, this category is problematic, because women vary greatly, depending on age, class, ethnic identity, sexual orientation, and so on.[33] If knowledge is the product of experience, we have to be absolutely clear that we cannot presume a unified experience, or set of experiences, across all women.

It is also problematic to undertake the task of articulating women's experience, silenced as it has traditionally been in patriarchal culture, in the categories, concepts, and language available. (This goes back to the problem with Kristeva's and others' argument about women speaking from the pre-Symbolic, discussed earlier.) The project of building a new, woman-centred knowledge totally outside the dominant culture seems to me to be a doomed one. For this reason, the strategy of 'destabilization', proposed by Sandra Harding, appears to be the most useful one at the moment. Such a deconstructive exercise, which operates by exposing the ideological limitations of male thought, begins to make space for women's voices and women's experience.

At this point we can come back to questions of women's writing and women's art. We find a similar opposition here, between those feminists who want their work to present a positive celebration of women's lives and women's identities (the art of Judy Chicago and Nancy Spero and the writing of Monique Wittig, for example), and those feminists who employ the various media to deconstruct dominant meanings, problematizing issues of gender and opening up spaces for women to articulate their experiences (for example, the work of Mary Kelly, Silvia Kolbowski, Barbara Kruger). The celebratory work, which often revives traditional female crafts (embroidery, quilting, flower-painting), or uses the female body itself as vehicle and subject-matter, is too often naïvely essentialist. Moreover, it misses the point that in a patriarchal culture it is not possible simply to declare a kind of unilateral independence. To go back to the vocabulary of feminist epistemology, we cannot just propose a 'successor art', which miraculously circumvents the dominant regime of representation. The guerrilla tactics of engaging with that regime and undermining it with 'destabilizing' strategies (collage, juxtaposition, re-appropriation of the image, and so on) provide the most effective possibility for feminist art practice today. This is partly a matter of strategy (because celebratory art, which does not engage in this way, often remains separate and is easily marginalized by the art establishment); and partly a matter of analytic understanding (because it simply is *not* possible to operate outside language). As we have seen, psychoanalytic approaches sometimes have their own difficulty with this, proposing a feminist language which is in some sense 'outside' language and culture. It is clear that the only responsible and coherent strategies now are those based on the more limited objective of engaging with, and destabilizing, the images, ideologies, and systems of representation of patriarchal culture. Women's writing and women's art, like women's knowledge, begins to articulate the silenced voice of women, but it is obliged to do so in the context of a dominant, alien, but ultimately enabling culture.

NOTES

1 Virginia Woolf, 'Women and Fiction', *Collected Essays*, vol. 1 (London, Hogarth Press, 1966).

2 Virginia Woolf, 'Dorothy Richardson', in *Collected Essays*. (See 'Feminism and Modernism' in this collection.)

3 Hélène Cixous, 'The Laugh of the Medusa', in Elaine Marks and Isabelle de Courtivron (eds), *New French Feminisms* (New York, Schocken Books, 1981).

4 Julia Kristeva, *Revolution in Poetic Language* (New York, Columbia University Press, 1984).

5 Lisa Tickner, 'Nancy Spero: Images of Women and *la peinture féminine*', in *Nancy Spero* (London, Institute of Contemporary Arts, 1987).

6 Jonathan Culler, *On Deconstruction: Theory and Criticism after Structuralism* (London, Routledge & Kegan Paul, 1983), ch. 1, Section 2: 'Reading as a Woman'.

7 Judith Fetterley, *The Resisting Reader* (Bloomington, Indiana University Press, 1978).

8 Elaine Showalter, 'Feminist Criticism in the Wilderness' in Elizabeth Abel (ed.), *Writing and Sexual Difference* (Brighton, Harvester Press, 1982), p. 14.

9 Edwin Ardener, 'Belief and the Problem of Women', in Shirley Ardener (ed.), *Perceiving Women* (London, J.M. Dent & Sons, 1975).

10 *Guardian* (19 May 1986), and *Spare Rib*, no. 168 (July 1986).

11 Showalter, 'Feminist Criticism in the Wilderness', p. 31.

12 David Morgan, 'Men, Masculinity and the Process of Sociological Enquiry', in Helen Roberts (ed.), *Doing Feminist Research* (London, Routledge & Kegan Paul, 1981).

13 Leonore Davidoff and Catherine Hall, *Family Fortunes: Men and Women of the English Middle Class, 1780–1850* (London, Hutchinson, 1987), pp. 32–4.

14 Dale Spender, *Man Made Language* (London, Routledge & Kegan Paul, 1980), quoted by Maria Black and Rosalind Coward, 'Linguistic, Social and Sexual Relations: A Review of Dale Spender's Man-Made Language', *Screen Education*, no. 39 (Summer 1981), p. 76.

15 Black and Coward, ibid.; Deborah Cameron, *Feminism and Linguistics* (London, Macmillan, 1985).

16 Kristeva, *Revolution in Poetic Language*, p. 29.

17 Ibid., p. 68. See also discussion in 'Reinstating Corporeality: Feminism and Body Politics' in this collection.

18 Ann Oakley and Robin Oakley, 'Sexism in Official Statistics', in John

Irvine *et al.* (eds), *Demystifying Social Statistics* (London, Pluto, 1979).

19   Ann Oakley, 'Interviewing Women: A Contradiction in Terms', in Roberts (ed.), *Doing Feminist Research*.

20   Morgan, 'Men, Masculinity and the Process of Sociological Enquiry', p. 86.

21   Dorothy Smith, 'Women's Perspective as a Radical Critique of Sociology', *Sociological Inquiry*, 44, (1974), p. 8.

22   Sandra Harding and Merrill B. Hintikka (eds), *Discovering Reality: Feminist Perspectives on Epistemology, Metaphysics, Methodology, and Philosophy of Science* (Dordrecht, D. Reidel, 1983), p. x.

23   Hilary Rose, 'Hand, Brain, and Heart: A Feminist Epistemology for the Natural Sciences', *Signs*, 9 (1983), p. 73.

24   Ibid.

25   Nancy Chodorow, *The Reproduction of Mothering: Psychoanalysis and the Sociology of Gender* (Berkeley, University of California Press, 1978); Dorothy Dinnerstein, *The Mermaid and the Minotaur* (New York, Harper & Row, 1976).

26   Nancy Hartsock, 'The Feminist Standpoint: Developing the Ground for a Specifically Feminist Historical Materialism', in Harding and Hintikka (eds), *Discovering Reality*, p. 295.

27   Ibid.

28   Evelyn Fox Keller, 'Gender and Science', in Harding and Hintikka (eds), *Discovering Reality*, p. 199.

29   Evelyn Fox Keller, *Reflections on Gender and Science* (New Haven, Conn., Yale University Press, 1985), pp. 10–11.

30   Jane Flax, 'Political Philosophy and the Patriarchal Unconscious: A Psychoanalytic Perspective on Epistemology and Metaphysics', in Harding and Hintikka (eds), *Discovering Reality*, p. 270.

31   Sandra Harding, *The Science Question in Feminism* (Ithaca, Cornell University Press, 1986), p. 194.

32   See Janet Wolff, 'The Critique of Reason and the Destruction of Reason', in Roy Landau (ed.), *The Relative and the Rational in the Architecture and Culture of the Present* (London, Architectural Association, forthcoming).

33   Harding, *Science Question in Feminism* p. 192.

6

Postmodern Theory and Feminist Art Practice

Postmodernism has been welcomed enthusiastically by many feminist artists and critics, frustrated by their continuing exclusion from the dominant modernist tradition in the visual arts. The particular strategies of postmodernist art practice are seen as potentially critical and radical interventions into what is still predominantly a patriarchal culture. Craig Owens, in one of the first of the now numerous collections of essays on postmodern theory, suggested the close affinity of feminism and postmodernism: 'The kind of simultaneous activity on multiple fronts that characterizes many feminist practices is a postmodern phenomenon.'[1]

This claim on behalf of recent developments in the visual arts has also been made with regard to so-called postmodernism in other media: for example dance, music, television, and popular culture. In this essay I shall review the arguments about the feminist potential of postmodern art, and consider some of the difficulties with this particular alliance.

The Failure of Modernism

Disillusion with modernism lies behind the optimism about postmodern cultural practices. Modernism was never, of course, a uniformly radical project. As Perry Anderson has pointed out, it was as diverse in its political affiliations as it was in its media, styles and manifestos.[2] But a central part of the modernist project was always avant-garde, in the sense of being both aesthetically and politically radical.[3] This project, however, in common with every movement in the history of art in the West, marginalized women and barred any possible feminist dimension, whether in painting and sculpture or in criticism.

Feminist art historians in the past fifteen years have achieved tremendous success in retrieving the work and lives of women artists from a history which managed to obliterate them from the record. Modernism is no exception to the general tendency of the art world to exclude women from production, and to refuse to acknowledge their work (in criticism, in art history) when they do paint. (This is discussed in more detail in 'Feminism and Modernism' in this collection.) The women artists among the early modernists are better known than they once were, thanks to the efforts of feminist historians: they include Berthe Morisot, Mary Cassatt, Suzanne Valadon, Rosa Bonheur. More recently the Surrealist movement has been reassessed, to rediscover the work of artists like Leonor Fini, Leonora Carrington, Lee Miller, Meret Oppenheim, and Frida Kahlo. The invisibility of women artists in the history of modernism reproduces that process whereby work by men (often the husbands or lovers of women artists) is taken seriously and that by women ignored: Frida Kahlo and Diego Rivera, Lee Krasner and Jackson Pollock are examples of this tendency to partial blindness on the part of art historians, and there are numerous others.

Part of the problem with modernism, then, has been the systematic exclusion of women from its institutions and its self-conception (see 'Feminism and Modernism'). There is little doubt that women are marginal to modernist art practice, which has become the dominant aesthetic in this century. The Tate Gallery in London, the Museum of Modern Art in New York, and the other major institutions of modernism in the visual arts produce and sustain a history of art which is mainly a history of the achievements of men. Women artists and feminist artists have recognized the closure of this arena, and turned elsewhere in order to engage critically with this establishment.

But it is not only feminists who have exposed the myth of the radical pretensions of modernism. There have always been those who have criticized the elitism of high modernism, and its denigration of all forms of mass or popular culture. The bureaucratization and institutionalization of modernism since the Second World War has been seen to coincide with its atrophying as a potentially critical movement.[4] The availability of Abstract

1 Ford Madox Brown, *Work*, (1852–65)

2 Augustus Leopold Egg, *Past and Present I* (1858)

3 Ernst Ludwig Kirchner, *Strasse mit roter Kokotte* (1914–25)

4 George Grosz, *Café* (1915)

5 August Macke, *Hutladen* (1913)

6 Gwen John, *Corner of the Artist's Room in Paris* (1907–10)

7 Mary Cassatt, *Susan on the Balcony Holding a Dog* (1883)

8 Edouard Vuillard, *Girl in an Interior* (1910)

9 Protest at Sandycove Bay, Dublin.

Expressionism for use in American propaganda in the Cold War has been cited as further evidence of the total collapse of the original project of modernism.[5] And it is clear that the most vehement defenders of modernism against both postmodernism and mass culture are critics of the right, for example those associated with the journal *New Criterion*.

The Promise of Postmodernism

If modernism no longer holds the promise of aesthetic and political transformation, postmodernism is often perceived as the new standard-bearer of the avant-garde. (The relationship between the two is complex, and depends both on the political evaluation of each category, and on whether postmodernism is seen as a continuation of modernism, or as a diametrically opposed phenomenon. The various possible permutations have been mapped out by Fredric Jameson.[6]) Here I shall consider the claims to the radical and critical perspective of postmodern culture in general, and specifically with regard to feminist art practice.

Postmodernism is seen as progressive because it operates outside the dominant, and moribund, academies of high modernism, and evades the bureaucratization and incorporation many have criticized in modernist work. Further, it blurs the boundaries between high art and popular culture, and enthusiastically takes advantage of the most up-to-date developments in technology, thus producing an anti-elitist and potentially democratic and accessible cultural form. Most important, postmodernism effects a 'critical deconstruction of tradition'.[7] Here postmodern cultural practice meets postmodern theory. The writings of Lyotard, Baudrillard, and Derrida, diverse though these are, definitively establish the impossibility of universalism in theory and the errors of any commitment to a notion of a transcendent (or at least accessible) Truth.

Given this critique, the radical task of postmodernism is to deconstruct apparent truths, to dismantle dominant ideas and cultural forms, and to engage in the guerrilla tactics of undermining closed and hegemonic systems of thought. This, more than anything else, is the promise of postmodernism for feminist politics. For the dominant discourses in our culture are invariably patriarchal, and it is the aim of postmodern feminist strategies to expose and discredit these. Craig Owens's suggestion of the close link between feminism and postmodernism, quoted at the beginning of this essay, is founded on this recognition.

It is not only in the arts that the potential of postmodernism for feminism has been recognized. American feminists who have been developing a critique of the natural sciences as partial and patriarchal practices have come to similar conclusions. The so-called objectivity of science has been shown by several writers to be a partial view, based on a projection of men's experience of the world. As the previous essay has shown, this has been explained in terms of a psychoanalytic account of the construction of masculinity in our culture, and in particular the need for males to develop a firm autonomy and detachment in the necessary break with the mother. (See 'Women's Knowledge and Women's Art'.) The critique of 'androcentric' knowledge leads to a debate about whether or not feminist approaches would entirely reject such notions of objectivity and attempts to develop theory, and, as I argued in that essay, to the realistic and politically useful conclusion of some feminists that we should adopt the middle path between radical relativism (anti-theory) and discredited universalism (totalizing theory). The proper role of such postmodern thought, acknowledging its own partiality, is one of an essentially deconstructive strategy. The inherently critical and destabilizing effects of postmodern theory make possible the direct engagement with androcentric systems of thought, without necessarily attempting to replace these with new, women-centred theories. The parallel with work in cultural studies and the arts is clear, for here too feminists have been arguing that deconstructive strategies are the most profitable.[8] Postmodern interventions, apart from anything else, achieve what a more separatist, alternative, woman-centred culture could not: namely engagement with the dominant culture itself. By employing the much-cited postmodern tactics of pastiche, irony, quotation, and juxtaposition, this kind of cultural politics engages directly with current images, forms, and ideas, subverting their intent and (re)appropriating their meanings, rather than abandoning them for alternative forms, which would leave them untouched and still dominant.

Problems of Postmodernism

There are a number of serious difficulties with this conception of postmodern theory and practice, and before going on to discuss postmodernism in the visual arts I want to consider two of these. The first, which is already apparent in the discussion of feminist science, is the problem of *theory*. For fundamental to the postmodern critique of metanarratives, dominant discourses, and so on, is the view that theories can no longer be seen as anything other than partial and provisional. Indeed, the development of structuralist and post-structuralist theory, hermeneutics, and the sociology of knowledge in recent decades has rendered impossible the retention of the view of science and knowledge which has lasted from the Enlightenment to Modernism, and which is founded on a faith in the uniformity of science and the possibility of a transcendent objectivity. In the late twentieth century we know that all knowledge is socially and historically located (and therefore partial), and that any theory is a product of (and limited by) language and discourse.

However, as several people have now pointed out, there is a certain inconsistency in this position. It has been argued that Lyotard's critique of theory is itself (necessarily) founded on theory.[9] Feminist postmodernism faces the same dilemma, because the deconstructive strategies of postmodern cultural practice, or of epistemological critique, depend on the theory of feminism – the articulated argument that society is structured around sexual inequality. Acknowledging this, Sandra Harding proposes replacing a confidently universal theory with a limited, provisional 'successor science'.[10] Nancy Fraser and Linda Nicholson have recently argued for the retention of 'large narratives', and for a postmodern-feminist theory which would be 'pragmatic and fallibilistic'.[11] But it has to be said that resolutions to this dilemma to date *are* mainly pragmatic. The epistemological paradox remains, and it may be that the justification of new critical theories can only be made on other, non-epistemological, grounds, including those of usefulness (one theory explains more of the world than another), politics (acknowledged commitment to a point of view), or self-reflexive provisionality (admission that this theory, though valuably deconstructive of dominant discourses, is itself open to such deconstruction).[12]

The second difficulty concerns the definition and identification of postmodernism itself. Although the history of the concept has been traced back at least to the 1950s, the introduction to a recent collection of essays on the topic can still conclude that 'there is, as yet, no agreed meaning to the term postmodern'.[13] The term has had particular currency in the 1980s, when the debates have ranged confusingly over a variety of media: literature, architecture, dance, painting, film, television, pop music video, dress, and fashion. It is often difficult to see how the concept transfers from one medium to another. The supposedly essential characteristics of postmodern art necessarily vary between media, leaving us more with an extremely elastic notion – a family of resemblances – than with a clearly identifiable category. To take one example of this: the demise of the unitary subject, central to postmodern film and literature, makes little sense in relation to architectural design.

The list of characteristics of postmodern culture is in any case a constantly shifting one. It includes pastiche, parody, historical quotation, depthlessness, loss of affect, decentring of the subject (but also, in the case of some so-called postmodern visual art, the resurrection of figurative art), eclecticism, self-reflexivity of the medium itself, and so on. The postmodern is also perceived by different writers as essentially aligned with quite varied, and sometimes opposed, political positions. Postmodern architecture has generally been seen as in some senses reactionary; postmodern dance, on the other hand, is associated with developments which are progressive (aesthetically and politically). This diversity within a category recalls Perry Anderson's warning about the complexities of modernism.[14] More, it suggests very strongly that the term, rather than describing and encapsulating a clearly visible phenomenon, is a construct of cultural critics, invented more for their own professional and ideological reasons than for its immediate usefulness. (A critical essay by Fred Orton and Griselda Pollock on the term 'Post-Impressionism' analyses a different historical moment and mercilessly deconstructs a similar catch-all but uncritical concept. For, as they argue, ' "Post-Impressionism" has no foundation in history and no pertinence to, or explanatory value for, that historical moment it is used to possess. . . . The use of the designation "Post-Impressionism" is part of a strategy to classify and contain diverse and complex practices and to blanket over difficulties and differences.'[15])

In addition, the term 'postmodernism' blurs important questions of periodization. The postmodern has variously been said to date from the Second World War, the 1950s, 1968, the late 1970s, and the 1980s. So far, few cultural critics have attempted to locate this cultural phenomenon within the particular social, economic, and historical transformations which have produced it. Jameson's now classic essay on postmodernism made a preliminary, though far too simplistic, attempt to do this in terms of broad periods of socio-economic development.[16] More recent contributions have started to take this further.[17] In general, though, the debate about the postmodern employs the quintessentially postmodern practice of detaching representation from reality. It is as if its critique of naïve conceptions of 'the real' justifies a blanket rejection of any further efforts in social and cultural history.

Lastly, the promiscuous use of the term 'postmodern' moves uneasily between the philosophical and the cultural. The debate about the 'postmodern condition' and about postmodernity, in which Lyotard's work has been central, concerns the epistemological question of the failure of the project of modernity – the recognition of the ultimate impossibility of grand narratives and of universal theories. The debate about postmodern*ism* as cultural practice, however, concerns the failure of modern*ism*, and the commitment to critical, fragmentary, democratic cultural politics. Of course there are links between the two discourses (postmodern cultural politics often relies on the advances of post-structuralist theory which underlie postmodern philosophy), but it is a mistake to assume any straightforward identity of the two. Many so-called postmodern art forms (for example, neo-classicism in painting and architecture) are far removed from, and indeed hostile to, the philosophically radical project of postmodern philosophy.

Given the complexities of the current debates about post-modernism, in what follows I shall concentrate on a relatively narrow area: postmodernism in painting. It will become clear that even here there is no easy definition of the postmodern. I shall begin by outlining the issues involved in the field of the visual arts, and go on to consider the potential for feminist art practice in postmodern painting.

Postmodernism and the Visual Arts

What is postmodern painting? In general in this area we find assumption rather than analysis, description rather than definition. As a result, there is no agreement on what constitutes postmodern painting. Fredric Jameson's infuential article on postmodernism discusses Andy Warhol's painting *Diamond Dust Shoes* as a key example of a postmodern work, contrasting this with the modernist

Van Gogh painting *Peasant Shoes*.[18] Waldemar Januszczak, in an overview of contemporary postmodernism in the visual arts, refers to neo-expressionist and neo-classical painters of the 1980s, including Kiefer, McKenna, Baselitz, Clemente, and Schnabel.[19] He does not define postmodern art, but refers to its characteristics of 'sensationalism, titillation, frilliness, pastiche, dumbness and narcissism' (which he compares with those same characteristics in Rococo painting). The sole ambition of postmodernism, he says, is to please. It has no moral ambition and no educational or creative purpose.

Charles Jencks, the main critic and defender of postmodern architecture, defines postmodernism as *double coding*, which he sees as at the same time the continuation and transcendence of modernism.[20] Postmodern art, he argues, started in about 1960 with Pop Art, Hyperrealism and other departures from modernism.[21] He pays particular attention to three Italian 'postmodern' painters: Carlo Maria Mariani, Sandro Chia, and Mimmo Paladino. He includes, in passing, David Hockney, Malcolm Morley, Eric Fischl, Lennart Anderson, Paul Georges, and Ron Kitaj, and a few others who 'make use of the classical tradition in portraying our current cultural situation'.[22] For Jencks, many of the painters described as 'postmodern' by other critics (including Jameson, Foster, and Owens, already mentioned in this essay) are not postmodern but rather 'late modern'. Missing in the work of such artists is the 'return to tradition' and to the 'classical' which is central to the double coding.

This conception of the postmodern is totally at variance with that of writers like Craig Owens. Owens's definition of postmodern art, unlike Jencks's, is work which undermines representation, and which operates a deconstructive action within art.[23] Artists he discusses include Martha Rosler, Mary Kelly, Barbara Kruger, Sherrie Levine, and Cindy Sherman. What these have in common, as well as a radical and feminist intention, is a theoretically informed interrogation of representation, including, in the case of the first three, the use of text and caption together with image. This is to return to a view of postmodern cultural practice which connects with poststructuralist and postmodern theory, and whose radical project is the destabilizing of the image.

Just as 'post-Impressionism' operates as an eclectic category, covering an enormous variety of styles and movements which have in common only the fact that they are 'after Impressionism', so 'postmodernism' in art appears to be a movable category whose only commitment is to identify what comes after modernism. For this reason, figurative painting has been called 'postmodern', since it reverses and challenges the orthodoxy of modernism (as established and maintained by the Museum of Modern Art in New York and, to some extent, the Tate Gallery in London). It is clear, though, that like postmodern architecture this could equally be a retrograde rather than progressive step. But whether painting is abstract or representational does not alone determine its political orientation. The rejection of modernism can be the rejection (from the right) of its original radical project, or the attempt (on the left) to revive that project in terms appropriate to the late twentieth century.

Given the confusion and lack of clarity of the debate in the field of painting, it is not surprising that one solution has been to suggest that there is more than one postmodernism. Hal Foster differentiates between a postmodernism of reaction and a postmodernism of resistance.[24] The debate between Habermas and his critics, too, seems to me to depend on opposite notions of the postmodern, Habermas's critique being of Foster's 'postmodernism of reaction'.[25] Of course, as is always the case when confronted with different uses of the same concept, the point is not to legislate for a 'correct' usage. The word means what people use it to mean. My own strategy, for the rest of this essay, will be to adopt a particular usage, and to assess postmodernism thus defined.

I would argue that the most useful definition of the postmodern, in painting as in other media, is that work which self-consciously deconstructs tradition, by a variety of formal and other techniques (parody, juxtaposition, re-appropriation of images, irony, repetition, and so on). Such an interrogation is informed by theoretical and critical consciousness. This definition excludes those other playful practices which fragment and disrupt narrative and tradition, and which refuse any grounding or closure in favour of a free play of signifiers. The critique of metanarratives notwithstanding, this disavowal of theory is unacceptable for two reasons. In the first place, cultural intervention as political critique is necessarily grounded in a particular analysis of social inequalities (as well as in a theoretical grasp *of* culture and the possibilities of its subversion). And in the second place there is always something disingenuous about the insistence on a free-floating critical consciousness, engaging in the guerrilla tactics of local disruption but uncontaminated by theory. There is always a point of view (theory), implicit if not explicit, which motivates and organizes such a critique.

In a recent review of the 'postmodern' television series, *State of the Art*, John Roberts has exposed this well.[26] The series abandoned the traditional documentary style of voice-over narrative and con-textualization of interviews and work. Roberts points out that the consequence of this was not only that those viewers without the relevant knowledge would find it difficult or impossible to grasp the 'relentless flow of uncontextualised information',[27] but that important differences were glossed over – facts about race, class, different economic positions of the artists, and so on. His sugges-tion that links between economic and critical success can be extrapolated, though they are not made explicit by the pro-grammes, indicates that despite the commitment to anti-narrative (postmodern) film strategies the makers of the programmes had a clear analysis, and the apparently random interviews, quotations and shots of paintings were in fact far from random.

This conception of postmodern art abandons the broad inclusive category of all painting which is after (or anti) modernism. It excludes neo-Expressionism and neo-Classicism, for even historical quotation (or double coding) is not postmodern if it is merely aimless play. The notion of the postmodern as informed, critical cultural practices which engage with tradition in order to subvert it brings us back to the consideration of postmodernism in feminist art practice.

Feminism and the Visual Arts

Deconstructive strategies are not the only kind of feminist artistic practice. Some feminist artists, like Judy Chicago, have chosen to make work which foregrounds women's history, women's lives, and women's traditional art and craft activities. In feminist art criticism there has been a good deal of debate about the virtues, limits, and dangers of such cultural politics – marginalization, essentialism, uncritical and undifferentiated notions of the (female) subject, and so on.[28] This essay, which focuses on postmodern cultural practices, should be seen in the context of a far wider range of feminist strategies. Some of the reservations which have been expressed about deconstructive practices, which I shall discuss

below, register an unwillingness to rule out other, less confron-
tational kinds of work.

Barbara Kruger has been quoted as saying 'I see my work as a
series of attempts to ruin certain representation, to displace the
subject and to welcome a female spectator into the audience of
men'.[29] Her work combines image and text, superimposing
accusatory texts onto black and white photographs.[30] The message,
often addressed to the male viewer, confronts society's construction
of women. 'We won't play nature to your culture', placed in large
irregular letters over an image of a woman's face, her eyes covered
by two leaves, both speaks of and challenges the traditional association of women with nature (and her exclusion from culture). The
intertextuality of her work subverts the patriarchal ideology of our
society by engaging directly with its representation, and subverting
this in ways which are inescapable.

Mary Kelly's monumental project, *Post-Partum Document*,
explores the mother-child relationship through text, diary, image,
and exhibited objects.[31] It is informed by Lacanian analysis of that
relationship, and, as Griselda Pollock has pointed out, rather than
producing 'a fixed coherent autobiographical work with an
integrated woman as its subject', it operates with fissure, fragment,
absence. For Pollock, this work epitomizes feminist art practices,
which are political 'because of the relations they do, or do not,
sustain to dominant discourses and modes of representation'.[32] Like
all work which is here being labelled 'postmodern', these practices
engage with representation in order to deconstruct the given
categories of gender and to reposition the spectator in relation to the
hitherto unquestioned images and ideologies of contemporary
culture. Mary Kelly's latest work, *Interim*, interrogates the
discourse of aging in patriarchal culture, again using text, image,
and object.[33]

An exhibition of 1985, entitled *Difference: On Representation
and Sexuality*, included the work of Kruger and Kelly among that of
twenty British and American artists. The exhibition was shown in
New York and London.[34] It included the work of a few men,
involved in exploring masculinity as part of the project of the
critique of the subject in culture and of the representation of gender
in contemporary society. Most of the work shown investigated the
relationship between text and image; all of it was committed to an
exploration of language and representation in the construction of
gendered subjects. Like an earlier show, curated by Mary Kelly

(*Beyond the Purloined Image* at the Riverside Studios, London, 1983), the exhibition was organized around the postmodern principle of deconstructing contemporary culture through art and representation.[35] The radical potential of an art practice which not only poses alternative images and ideologies, but refuses pre-existent and unitary categories of 'woman' and 'feminine', is clear.

However, some feminist art critics have taken issue with the apparent centrality of postmodernism, particularly in the context of British feminist art. Unlike the United States, where there is a more liberal pluralism of art practices among feminists, postmodern, deconstructive art has become something of an orthodoxy, which is resented as both intimidating and exclusive by artists working in humanist and other traditions. A frequent objection to feminist deconstructionism is its relative inaccessibility; a knowledge of Freud, Lacan and post-structuralist theory often seems a prerequisite to understanding the work. Angela Partington has argued against the notion of a 'correct' textual strategy in feminist art, partly on these grounds.[36] Her article is a plea for an audience-centred art practice, which stresses *extra*-textual strategies (taking into account the actual relations of artistic production and consumption). Deconstruction gives priority to the producer-text relationship at the expense of the consumer-text relationship. Humanist or celebratory strategies (Nancy Spero, Judy Chicago, Sylvia Sleigh, Susan Hiller, Miriam Schapiro are mentioned, among others) enable a shared experience of 'the feminine' in a way which, she claims, need not be essentialist (that is, illegitimately ahistorical and non-social). Deconstructive strategies, on the other hand, as a primarily textual strategy ignore audiences and viewers, and opt for formal critique instead of engagement with women's actual social position and viewing practices.

Katy Deepwell documents and criticizes the dominance of deconstructive work (which she terms 'scripto-visual'). Characteristic of this work, she says, is a rejection of painting in favour of photography, film, video, performance. She writes in favour of continuing to allow those other feminist practices, mainly based on painting, by artists 'who believe in a coherent humanist subject "woman" and embrace woman-centred, and *sometimes* essentialist, views about a separate female culture in their work'.[37] Artists she mentions include Judy Chicago, Rose Garrard, Nancy Spero, and Therese Oulton. In passing she also makes the point that black women's practices are ignored by the scripto-visual ascendancy, and it has indeed emerged in a number of recent debates among feminists that black women artists in Britain show few signs of allegiance to deconstructive practices.

Rosa Lee makes a different case against deconstruction as feminist art.[38] Against the representational strategies of postmodern art, she counterposes the possibility of non-representational art as potentially radical. (Her main example is the work of Therese Oulton – large landscape-like abstract canvases.) Like Katy Deepwell, she stresses the importance of working with (or returning to) oil paint and the gestural mark. Engagement with the material language of the medium itself is central, in which the subversive act consists in the use of traditional conventions without the representational (and perhaps compromised) content which might be expected. Her objection to deconstructive postmodernism seems to be mainly to its hegemony within the women's art movement, to its marginalization of painting, and to the fact that it therefore does not allow the possibility of a radical reconstruction of artistic language.

A final objection to postmodernism as feminist art practice is that it might not, after all, be achieving its radical cultural and political aims. Barbara Creed, in a discussion of postmodernism and film, suggests that the crisis of the master narratives may not necessarily benefit women.[39] Rosa Lee argues that 'the choices and "options" supposedly up for grabs within postmodernism are available only for the male of the species'.[40] And Griselda Pollock warns against the temptation for feminist artists to abandon modernist strategies in favour of postmodernism.[41] I shall conclude by assessing the prospects of deconstructive postmodernism as feminist art practice in the late twentieth century.

Postmodernism as Modified Modernism

Tactically, celebratory feminist art may well connect with viewers' experience and mobilize a certain critical consciousness. To that extent, Partington and Deepwell are right to object to the more authoritarian rejection of such humanist work by deconstructionists. They are also right to insist that cultural political strategies cannot be purely textual ones; that any such intervention must be judged in terms of the specific circumstances of viewers, contemporary meanings, potential (mis)interpretations (including by critics) and so on. However, the major difference between postmodernism, as I have been using the term, and other kinds of feminist art practice is the commitment of the former to engage critically with contemporary culture and with the very categories of gender themselves. To that extent, there is no question of a liberal plurality of feminist strategies, since such work is clearly fundamentally radical in a way that other work is not. It is arguable, too, that since it does engage in this way with dominant cultural forms, re-appropriating and subverting imagery, it may be less likely to be marginalized and ignored in the way that woman-centred art generally is.

It is true that the majority of the work I have been discussing under the heading of deconstructive postmodernism has abandoned painting in favour of photography and other visual forms. Unlike Lee, I do not think it has to be a central project of feminist art to reconstruct the traditional language of art (namely oil paint), though there is no real reason why postmodern art cannot employ paint as well as photography (except for the obvious one that mechanically reproduced images lend themselves more to fragmentation, re-arrangement, superimposition, and other deconstructive strategies). The medium itself is not essentially compromised in a way which excludes feminist appropriation, as the work of artists like Alexis Hunter, Susan Hiller, and Sutapa Biswas shows.

As for the warning that postmodernism may be co-opted by men, the immediate and pragmatic answer must be that feminists should nevertheless employ those strategies as long as they are available and as long as they seem effective. It has been true throughout the history of western art that all major art movements have been dominated by men (and also that the part played in them by women has been written out of the historical account). This does not seem to be a good reason for abdicating in advance. The deconstructive strategies of postmodern cultural practice are invaluable for feminists, and a realistic politics for artists is one that judges the availability and effectivity of particular strategies in the moment.

I return finally to the question of theory. It has often occurred to me that the characteristics of so-called postmodernism appear to duplicate many of those adduced more than half a century ago in relation to modernism: self-reflexivity, de-centring of the subject, alienation-effect, consciousness of, and attention to, the medium itself, montage, use of new media, and so on. If anything, the key difference was the reliance of modernism on theory, whether this was Marxism (in the case of Brecht and some of the Russian Futurists) or other theories of industrial society and social change. Since the development of structuralist, semiotic and discourse theories, postmodernism has claimed to be based on a rejection of grand theory. But as I have already argued, this rejection of theory is inconsistent and ultimately indefensible. Although we may now have a less naïve view of objectivity, recognizing the inevitably perspectival nature of any theory, postmodernism cannot be atheoretical any more than modernism.

It is for this reason that I want to conclude by suggesting that the best kind of postmodern theory and practice is in fact a kind of modified modernism. To understand this we have to detach the project of modernism from its fate in terms of particular institutions of art and culture. The so-called failure of modernism is, of course, the impasse it reached as a result of certain processes of bureaucratization, institutionalization, and commercialization. As Griselda Pollock has argued recently, we must separate modernism-as-institution from modernism-as-practice.[42] The latter is by no means a monolithic entity, and it is thus still available for radical initiatives. She doubts that postmodernism is a real aesthetic break from modernism, and in another essay she argues strongly in favour of Brechtian modernism, whose 'theoretical and practical contributions for a political art practice remain a valid and necessary component of the contemporary women's art movement'.[43]

Postmodern theory and postmodern cultural practices have a good deal to offer feminist artists and critics. As I have argued however, the radical relativism and scepticism of much postmodern thought is misplaced, unjustified, and incompatible with feminist (and indeed any radical) politics. The project of postmodernism as cultural politics is more usefully seen as a renewal and continuation of the project of modernism, and the specific strategies, techniques, and technologies of the late twentieth century enable the energetic and constantly innovatory pursuit of a feminist art practice.

NOTES

1 Craig Owens, 'The Discourse of Others: Feminism and Post-modernism', in Hal Foster (ed.), *Postmodern Culture* (London, Pluto, 1985), p. 63.

2 Perry Anderson, 'Modernity and Revolution', *New Left Review*, 144 (March/April 1984).
3 See Eugene Lunn, *Marxism and Modernism: An Historical Study of Lukács, Brecht, Benjamin, and Adorno* (London, Verso, 1985).
4 Suzi Gablik, *Has Modernism Failed?* (London, Thames & Hudson, 1984).
5 Eva Cockcroft, 'Abstract Expressionism: Weapon of the Cold War', *Artforum*, 12, no. 10 (1974); Serge Guilbaut, *How New York Stole the Idea of Modern Art: Abstract Expressionism, Freedom, and the Cold War* (Chicago and London, University of Chicago, 1983).
6 Fredric Jameson, 'The Politics of Theory: Ideological Positions in the Postmodernism Debate', *New German Critique*, 33 (1984). (Special issue on *Modernity and Postmodernity*.)
7 Hal Foster, 'Postmodernism: A Preface', in *Postmodern Culture* (London, Pluto, 1985), p. xii.
8 Angela McRobbie, 'Postmodernism and Popular Culture', in Lisa Appignanesi (ed.), *Postmodernism* (ICA Documents 4; London, Institute of Contemporary Arts, 1986); E. Ann Kaplan, *Rocking around the Clock: Music Television, Postmodernism, and Consumer Culture* (London, Methuen, 1987); Chris Weedon, *Feminist Practice and Poststructuralist Theory* (Oxford, Blackwell, 1987).
9 Axel Honneth, 'An Aversion against the Universal: A Commentary on Lyotard's *Postmodern Condition*', *Theory, Culture & Society*, 2, no. 3 (1985) (special issue on *The Fate of Modernity*); Douglas Kellner, 'Postmodernism as Social Theory: Some Challenges and Problems', *Theory, Culture & Society*, 5, nos 2–3 (1988) (special issue on *Postmodernism*).
10 Sandra Harding, *The Science Question in Feminism* (Ithaca, NY, and London, Cornell University Press, 1986).
11 Nancy Fraser and Linda Nicholson, 'Social Criticism without Philosophy: An Encounter between Feminism and Postmodernism', *Theory, Culture & Society*, 5, nos 2–3 (1988), pp. 380, 391. (Special issue on *Postmodernism*.)
12 Janet Wolff, 'The Critique of Reason and the Destruction of Reason', in Roy Landau (ed.), *The Relative and the Rational in the Architecture and Culture of the Present* (London, Architectural Association, forthcoming).
13 Mike Featherstone, 'In Pursuit of the Postmodern: An Introduction', *Theory, Culture & Society*, 5, nos 2–3 (1988), p. 207. (Special issue on *Postmodernism*.)
14 Anderson, 'Modernity and Revolution'.
15 Fred Orton and Griselda Pollock, 'Les Données Bretonnantes: la prairie de representation', *Art History*, 3, no. 3 (1980), p. 314.
16 Fredric Jameson, 'Postmodernism, or the Cultural Logic of Late Capitalism', *New Left Review*, 146 (1984).
17 John Tagg, 'Postmodernism and the Born-Again Avant-Garde', *Block*, 11 (1985/6); and Zygmunt Bauman, 'Is There a Postmodern

Sociology?'; Philip Cooke, 'Modernity, Postmodernity and the City'; and Sharon Zukin, 'The Postmodern Debate over Urban Form', in *Theory, Culture & Society*, 5, nos 2–3 (1988) (special issue on *Postmodernism*).

18 Jameson, 'Postmodernism', pp. 58–60.
19 Waldemar Januszczak, 'Decline and Fall of Modern Art', *Guardian* (2 December 1986).
20 Charles Jencks, *What Is Post-Modernism?* (London, Academy Editions, 1986), pp. 14–15.
21 Ibid., p. 23.
22 Ibid., p. 30.
23 Owens, 'The Discourse of Others'.
24 Foster, 'Postmodernism: A Preface'.
25 Jürgen Habermas, 'Modernity versus Postmodernity', *New German Critique*, 22 (1981) (special issue on *Modernism*); Richard J. Bernstein (ed.), *Habermas and Modernity* (Cambridge, Polity Press, 1985).
26 John Roberts, 'Postmodern Television and the Visual Arts', *Screen*, 28, no. 2 (1987).
27 Ibid., p. 124.
28 See for example Judith Barry and Sandy Flitterman, 'Textual Strategies: The Politics of Art-Making', *Screen*, 21, no. 2 (1980).
29 Barbara Kruger, Press Release (New York, Annina Nosei Gallery, 1984).
30 Barbara Kruger, *We Won't Play Nature to your Culture* (London, Institute of Contemporary Arts, 1983).
31 Mary Kelly, *Post-Partum Document* (London, Routledge & Kegan Paul, 1983).
32 Griselda Pollock, 'Feminism and Modernism', in Rozsika Parker and Griselda Pollock (eds), *Framing Feminism: Art and the Women's Movement 1970–1985* (London, Pandora, 1987), p. 98.
33 Mary Kelly, *Interim* (Edinburgh, The Fruitmarket Gallery, 1986).
34 Paul Smith, 'Difference in America', *Art in America* (April 1985); *Difference: On Representation and Sexuality* (New York, The New Museum of Contemporary Art, 1984).
35 Mary Kelly, 'Beyond the Purloined Image', *Block*, 9 (1983).
36 Angela Partington, 'Feminist Art and Avant-Gardism', in Hilary Robinson (ed.), *Visibly Female: Feminism and Art Today* (London, Camden Press, 1987), and 'Conditions of a Feminist Art Practice', *Feminist Arts News*, 2, no. 4 (n.d.).
37 Katy Deepwell, 'In Defence of the Indefensible: Feminism, Painting and Post-Modernism', *Feminist Arts News*, 2, no. 4 (n.d.), p. 11.
38 Rosa Lee, 'Resisting Amnesia: Feminism, Painting and Postmodernism', *Feminist Review*, no. 26 (1987).
39 Barbara Creed, 'From Here to Modernity – Feminism and Postmodernism', *Screen*, 28, no. 2 (1987), p. 66.
40 Lee, 'Resisting Amnesia', p. 8.

41 Pollock, 'Feminism and Modernism', p. 104.
42 Ibid., p. 106.
43 Griselda Pollock, 'Screening the Seventies: Sexuality and Representation in Feminist Practice – A Brechtian Perspective', in *Vision and Difference: Femininity, Feminism and Histories of Art* (London, Routledge, 1988), p. 199.

7

Texts and Institutions: Problems
of Feminist Criticism

The development of interdisciplinary approaches to the study of literature and the other arts has been a major advance in British and American scholarship in the past fifteen or twenty years. It has meant the provision of a conceptual framework in which we could move from a narrow, and historically and politically uncritical, focus on a succession of Texts and Writers, to a more adequate understanding and interpretation of literary works and practices. As a result, it becomes possible to address such issues as the production, in specific social and historical circumstances, of the 'great tradition' itself, the origin and significance of the hierarchy of genres and styles (high art, popular culture, and so on), and the relationship between modes of representation and structures of cultural production and reception. Questions of aesthetic value can no longer be simply a matter of assertion, faith, or uncritical traditional assumption, but are themselves subjected to social and political scrutiny. This is not, needless to say, to import politics into the pure realm of the aesthetic; it is to expose the pretence of political innocence in the mainstream of literature and criticism.

One of the questions I shall want to pursue in this essay is the actual extent of cross-disciplinary collaboration in the study of culture. My central argument is that current work is still inhibited and limited by the lack of a real interdisciplinarity; and, moreover, that this limitation is evident in the case of feminist literary criticism. Specifically, I shall argue that the two approaches, of textual critique and of sociological analysis of the institutions of cultural production, must be combined if we are to produce a

comprehensive feminist account of literature which can link conditions of production (women as authors, for example) with
characteristics of representation (narrative and literary conventions
as constituting and limiting the presentation of women in the text).
To date, literary approaches and sociological approaches have
developed as quite distinct. My argument is that we cannot properly
understand texts apart from their institutional and social origins;
and that, conversely, institutional analyses (of writers, publishers,
libraries, criticism, and so on) are inadequate unless they are also
able to address questions of textuality. In the case of feminist
literary criticism, we need a sensitive and careful critical analysis of
textual representation in the context of a social-historical grasp of
the processes and institutions in which literature is produced and
consumed.

It is worth starting with a rehearsal of the advantages already
gained from the weakening of discipline boundaries, in the development of new areas of study and teaching (communication and
cultural studies, humanities programmes, women's studies, media
studies), and in the birth of regular conferences and journals as
forums for discussion of this work (*Literature and History* and
Media, Culture & Society in Britain, *Cultural Critique* and *Social
Text* in the United States, *Thesis Eleven* in Australia, and many
others). From the point of view of literary studies, contact and
cooperation with sociologists, historians, and analysts of popular
cultural forms has enabled a new and crucial critical perspective.[1]
(And it is worth pointing out that parallel developments in other
traditional humanities disciplines, notably art history and, more
recently, music, have not only provided the possibility of major
revisions of those areas, but also offered the opportunity to explore
the 'inter-textuality' *across* the arts.[2]) From the point of view of the
social sciences, until fairly recently more interested in economic,
industrial, and political areas of society than in the history or
sociology of culture, it has meant a broader understanding of the
totality of social life.[3] Last, with regard to the developing sociology
of the arts, which now has a history of about twenty years in both
Britain and the United States[4], insofar as sociologists have
increasingly had access to the ideas and work of literary (and art)
critics they have been in a position to pay more careful attention to
textuality and representation, rather than simply taking texts as
unproblematic (and unexplored) entities which only needed to be
related in some way to social structure and process. (However, as I

go on to argue in this essay, sociologists have not taken enough advantage of this opportunity.)

Women's studies has, since its very inception, been interdisciplinary. Indeed, one could say that the oppression of women – in society as in intellectual history – has depended amongst other things on the clear separation and segregation of disciplines. As the editors of a volume of essays on women's studies have put it, 'there are plenty of good reasons, both political and academic, for using the study of women and sexual divisions to reflect on traditional disciplinary boundaries.'[5] There has, of course, been an enormous amount of important feminist work within the specific disciplines, concerned to 'bring women back' into areas of knowledge in which they have been marginalized or rendered invisible; hence the (re)discovery of women's history, of women artists and their work, of those areas of social life traditionally ignored by the social sciences, not least because women rather than men have occupied them (the so-called private arena of the home, those categories of employment in which women predominate, and so on). But the separation of academic disciplines only mirrors and reinforces the separation of spheres of social life, and it is through this separation that gender differences and inequalities are maintained. Thus orthodoxies about women's (and men's) proper role, defended by historical generalization, have had to be questioned when confronted by the evidence of anthropologists about gender roles in other societies. The nature of the contemporary labour market, still essentially organized in terms of a fundamental sex segregation, can only be understood fully when analysed in relation to the nature of the family in modern society and, further, in conjunction with psychoanalytic explanations of the formation of gender identities within the family. The nature of representation of women in painting and in literature, already comprehensively documented and criticized by feminist scholars, must be considered in relation to the conditions and structures of cultural production and consumption (who *are* the artists, and what are the circumstances which enable their work and success?), as well as to broader areas of ideology and social relations.

What does this mean for feminist literary criticism? In the first place, the initial line of attack of feminists working in literary criticism and teaching in departments of literature was necessarily the critical reading of texts. This involved exposing the limited, and limiting, array of female stereotypes which have operated in literature;[6] undertaking studies of particular authors and texts in order to make explicit their patriarchal content;[7] analysing the dominant narrative structures which collude in the ideological containment of women;[8] and deciphering the various subversive strategies and elements employed (usually unconsciously) by women writers to represent alternatives to, or attacks on, the patriarchy,[9] as well as similarly subversive strategies available to contemporary readers of texts, including (or perhaps specifically) those by men.[10] This work has often been interdisciplinary, though in a fairly limited way, for example in connecting literary with visual representation[11], or employing psychoanalytic methods and concepts in literary analysis[12]. It has developed a valuable literature of critical studies, and an increasingly refined approach to the major texts of the literary canon (and also, incidentally, to the texts of popular literary forms[13]).

This approach has recently been criticized by feminists working in a rather different theoretical tradition, in a dialogue which is sometimes posed as an opposition between American liberal feminism and British socialist feminism,[14] and sometimes as an opposition between Anglo-American humanism and French theoreticism.[15] I will return to this debate later. But my main argument here is that this tradition of textual critique does not take full advantage of the interdisciplinary possibilities of women's studies; moreover, recent attempts to combine this approach with the more radical critique of language and analysis of sexual difference[16] have also, to date, failed to provide the comprehensive analysis of gender and writing which a fully interdisciplinary sociology of literature can make possible. In short, what is still missing is an approach which investigates *both* texts *and* institutions.

Alongside feminist work which has concentrated on the critique of existing texts there has also been another development, of feminist writing whose object is the rediscovery of women writers and the identification of the particular characteristics of women's writing.[17] (This has its parallel, in a more systematically developed form, in feminist art history, which has, amongst other things, sought to rediscover and reinstate the many women artists obliterated from the historical record.[18]) This shift from text to author is important, because it raises the possibility of engaging with those crucial *extra*-textual factors which constitute and determine the writing itself. It is the first step towards the explanation of patriarchal ideology and gender representation in texts, inasmuch as it directs attention to women's actual position in the social world. This is not to say that feminist critics looking at women's writing – or what Elaine Showalter has called 'gyno-critics'[19] – have always been interested in pursuing this question; for the most part, they have been content to limit themselves to brief and general overviews of women's relationship to literary produc-tion and their location in social structures, and perhaps to biographical detail concerning specific women authors.[20] This is where, in my view, a more thoroughly sociological approach is urgently needed. It is only with a systematic analysis of sexual divisions in society, of the social relations of cultural production, and of the relationship between textuality, gender and social structure that feminist literary criticism will really be adequate to its object.

In order to substantiate this claim, I want to return for a moment to considering the sociology of literature as a cross-disciplinary collaboration between sociologists and literary critics. There is no doubt that many of the most interesting and important contribu-tions to literary scholarship in recent years have resulted from the intervention of literary historians and literary critics committed to the perception of literature as a social product, and therefore to the critique and overthrow of the ideology of the autonomy of art. Their readings of texts have thus been sociological to the extent that they grasp literary representation as ideological (in the sense of being constituted by meanings, conventions, and forms of narrative which are systematically related to social-structural factors and extra-aesthetic power relations). Also sociological is that work by literary scholars which has helped to expose the mechanisms by which the very structures of the literary establishment (journals, criticism, educational institutions) combine to construct the myth of aesthetic autonomy.[21] But for the most part, critical literary criticism has concentrated on textual critique – sociologically and politically informed, but nevertheless incomplete in an important sense. In 1976 Terry Eagleton proposed a model for the analysis of literature, in which literary texts were understood as representing aesthetic ideologies (the dominant literary conventions of the time), authorial ideology (the writer's own social position as also relevant to the work), and general ideology (the class, and other systems of belief in which the works are produced).[22] He also insisted on the importance of paying attention to what he called the 'literary mode of production', by which he meant the institutional factors in which and through which texts are produced, distributed, and consumed. These would include publishers, libraries, printers, reviewers, critics, journals in which novels are serialized, and also associated legal and other factors (like copyright law, censorship, and so on). Eagleton stresses the centrality of the literary mode of production (LMP) to the text itself.

> It is important to note that the character of an LMP is a significant constituent of the literary product itself. We are not merely concerned here with the sociological outworks of the text; we are concerned rather with how the text comes to be what it is because of the specific determinations of its mode of production. If LMPs are historically extrinsic to particular texts, they are equally internal to them: the literary text bears the impress of its historical mode of production as surely as any product secretes in its form and materials the fashion of its making. . . . The character of an LMP is an internal constituent rather than merely an extrinsic limit of the character of the text.[23]

Eagleton has been one of the most influential exponents of the new 'critical' criticism, and yet this particular argument has been more or less ignored by writers who have enthusiastically taken up his proposals for the investigation of literature as ideology, and who have followed (and sometimes engaged critically with) his developing theories in subsequent books. In his own book on Richardson[24] he does look at this writer's work (and notably *Clarissa*) in relation to the literary mode of production in eighteenth-century England, and to Richardson's specific location within the relations of this system – as a printer, as a publisher of journals, and as a member of particular literary circles. The textual reading is then produced in conjunction with a more sociological conception of textual production. Raymond Williams, another key figure in the transformation of traditional English criticism, has also argued that culture (and hence literature) has to be analysed in terms of institutions as well as in terms of representation (even going so far – unusually for a literary critic – as to call this approach, and his own work, a '*sociology* of culture').

> A *sociology* of culture must concern itself with the institutions and formations of cultural production. . . . A sociology of *culture* must also concern itself with the social relations of its specific means of production. . . . It must further concern itself with the ways in which, within

social life, 'culture' and 'cultural production' are socially identified and distinguished. . . . A sociology of culture must further and most obviously concern itself with specific artistic forms. . . . In this area there is overlap with critical analysis and with the general study of sign-systems, as in semiotics.[25]

Again, Williams's own work has often exemplified this model well, analysing texts in relation to social and literary/cultural structures and processes.[26] And yet, despite the influential role played by both Williams and Eagleton in the new literary criticism, it remains the case that the majority of studies in what I have been referring to as 'critical' criticism are textual analyses. They are interpretations informed by an ideological-critical perspective, and hence necessarily sensitive to social and political factors. But they are rarely readings which attempt to discuss representation as the complex product of processes and institutions.

The opposite criticism can be levelled at the sociology of litera-ture as undertaken by sociologists. Cross-disciplinary collaboration here too disguises an ultimate unwillingness to engage in a fully *inter*disciplinary project. If literary critics focus on texts to the exclusion of institutions, sociologists analyse institutions without a real sensitivity to representation and textuality. Within the sociological literature, it is still too often the case that we can find interesting and original accounts of the institutions of publishing, patronage, and reading, and of the book market in general, which ignore entirely the *nature* of the literary work(s) in question.[27] I think it is fair to say that this textual agnosticism is more character-istic of the sociology of the arts in the United States than of work in Britain; the so-called production-of-culture approach to the arts in the United States has been much more firmly located *within* sociology, and less interdisciplinary, than equivalent work in Britain.[28] To some extent the tendency to take texts for granted, and to avoid any analysis or discussion of them *as* texts, is the conse-quence of the longstanding, and misguided, social scientific concern with 'objectivity' – manifest in this case in a careful circumvention of questions of aesthetics and literary value.[29] In other cases, such partial analyses of cultural products are simply based on the kind of narrowness and ignorance encouraged and sustained by the dominant, persistent, and totally artificial segregation of disciplines imposed by the professionalization of intellectual work and by our educational institutions. Whatever the reason, the practice of sociologists of culture and of literature who privilege institutional analysis over textual critique produces a sociology of literature which is not merely incomplete, but fundamentally distorted.[30] It is not just a question of linking social process with aspects of style.[31] More crucially, sociologistic methods permit and even encourage reductionist, and reflectionist, theories of literature; they are blind to the constitutive nature of culture itself (that is, to the recognition that social and ideological meanings are produced as much at the level of culture as in the 'real' relations of social and economic life); and they are totally unable to explain *why* it is certain works of literature that are produced, read, and validated in the specific circumstances under examination.[32]

My argument, then, is that the study of literature must be *both* at the level of texts *and* at the level of institutions and social process. It follows that a feminist approach to literature, profoundly committed as it must be to a sociological and political perspective, must also operate at both levels. (Even this formulation has unfortunate connotations of two separate tasks to be done. Rather, it is a matter of developing a complex method which is in effect a synthesis of existing approaches.) The interdisciplinary impulse of women's studies should facilitate such a development. Earlier I discussed some of the recent developments in feminist literary criticism, arguing that to date these have been restricted to textual critique and to exploring the characteristics of women's writing. Feminist sociologists have also begun to produce some fascinating work on the exclusionary effects of literary institutions for women writers. For example, Gaye Tuchman and Nina Fortin have analysed the records of the English publisher, Macmillans, in the nineteenth century, and demonstrated how, as a result of discriminatory practices, particularly by publishers' readers, women were gradually edged out of the literary market.[33] This kind of work is the essential complement to feminist textual analysis, for it is only possible to understand the patriarchal nature of literary representation (as well as the possibility in writing for women's oppositional voice) by scrutinizing the production of those texts in particular relations and institutions, literary, social, and political.

A good deal of current work in feminist literary criticism is structured around a particular debate, sometimes formulated as an implacable opposition between two approaches. This has recently been discussed in a careful and thorough exposition by Toril Moi.[34] She analyses, on the one hand, 'Anglo-American' feminist criticism, which she characterizes as a liberal-humanist approach, politically committed and challenging literary institutions, while failing to confront the questions of textuality and of sexual difference (as constituted in language and culture); and on the other hand, the 'French' tradition of feminist criticism, anti-humanist (in the sense of deconstructing the subject), committed to radical textual practice, but with a dangerous tendency to 'essentialism' (femininity as universal rather than cultural) and a lack of awareness of the social, and extra-textual, arena of sexual politics. It appears to be accepted by an increasing number of feminist critics that both developments are important, but that neither alone is adequate.[35] However, this division, which I referred to earlier, is *not* the same as the separation between the focus on texts and the focus on institutions (or between the literary and the sociological) with which this essay is primarily concerned. It is worth looking at, nevertheless, both because Moi's critique is an important contribution to the development of an adequate textual analysis, which must overcome the limitations of each of the traditions she considers, and also because there is a way in which she does appear to resolve the antinomy of text/institution: the Anglo-American approach in her account, for example, is described as challenging literary institutions, and being aware of extra-textual factors. However, although Toril Moi refers to the 'institutional critique' of Anglo-American work, she means by this 'the patriarchal mechanisms at work within the literary institution'.[36] There is no suggestion that this work addresses in a systematic way the historical development and contemporary structure and operation of literary institutions, or the complex array of mediators, practices, ideologies, and power relations of these institutions, and their location within, and interaction with, the broader social structure. As I have already argued, 'Anglo-American' feminist critics have not taken on the examination of social (and even cultural) processes and institutions in an adequately sociological way. In this, despite the more advanced social and historical perspective displayed (compared with the 'French' tradition), criticism is still essentially about texts and their characteristics.

My argument in this essay has been for a feminist literary criticism which is more thoroughly sociological (and for a feminist sociology of literature which is sensitive to its object). As a tentative model for what such work might be like, and how we might begin to go about it, we can consider recent contributions to feminist art criticism and, particularly, feminist film criticism. I referred earlier to the work of feminists who have rediscovered a whole tradition of women painters, ignored by the mainstream of art history, and obliterated from the historical record. Another important area of feminist work has been the critical analysis of representation in painting, and in particular the gender ideology which produces patriarchal stereotypes (of nude, of siren, of wife, of madonna, and so on) and which is in turn produced *by* them.[37] As with feminist literary criticism, less attention has been paid so far to the structures of artistic production as integrally related to visual representation, although some feminist art historians have described the operation of such structures in excluding (and occasionally facilitating) the participation and success of women.[38] Victor Burgin, whose photographic and theoretical work has been concerned with gender and sexuality, has also made clear the connection between represen-tation and (art) institution. In an interview he explained

I consider my work to consist of my interventions across the art institu-tion as a whole: across teaching, writing theory, sitting on committees, giving public talks, taking part in symposia, and so on. The reason I do all this is in an effort to help shift the ground of the institution as a whole.[39]

He continues

In the seventies, the preliminary attention was to 'images of women' – the 'stereotype', conceived of as an *image fixe*. This was, and still is, a necessary attention, but it can't be sufficient; the facts of representa-tion / sexuality don't just concern the *item*, the 'iconogramme', the facts are *articulated* – we're dealing with a *rhetoric* of sexuality; a rhetoric, moreover, embedded in, encountered in terms of, the entire social system (intertextual, institutional – *discursive*).[40]

The last statement, in particular, emphasizes the interplay of the textual and the extra-textual. For the project of a feminist art history is not just the critical study of representation; nor is it merely an account of women artists and their work. Even work which connects the two is limited inasmuch as it fails to comprehend both texts and artists within the complex system of aesthetic and ideological discourses, institutions and structures in which they reside. Art history, like literary criticism, is obliged to incorporate the best of the sociology of culture, which will enable the necessary attention to social process and cultural institutions.

Griselda Pollock, in a number of articles, has demonstrated the clear, if complex, relationship between woman as cultural producer and woman as 'sign'. She argues that the sexist and patriarchal social relations in art schools in Britain, which continue to disadvantage women students and women artists, are inseparable from the ideological and representational characteristics of dominant (and primarily modernist) modes of painting. The patriarchal nature of texts and the patriarchal nature of art institutions are totally interdependent, and they reproduce one another. Both are sustained by the ideology of individualism, which, as Pollock shows, in effect can only identify and refer to *male* subjects.[41] Griselda Pollock, with Deborah Cherry, has also shown how, in the case of the Pre-Raphaelite artist and model, Elizabeth Siddall, visual and written texts of the 1850s and since have jointly produced a definition of 'woman' and of femininity which occlude and obliterate the real circumstances of Elizabeth Siddall's biography, class origins, and art practice. Here, too, institutional and textual practices collude in the creation and retention of a patriarchal culture.[42]

In 1980 the feminist film critic, Claire Johnston, argued that 'while the emphasis on textual analysis in feminist film criticism has been productive . . . theoretical work on the relationship between text and subject and the historical conjuncture is now more important'.[43] Her main concern is to go beyond textual analysis to an examination of the conditions of *viewing* – that is, to the question of how texts are interpreted in specific historical and social circumstances. In other words, her interest is more in consumption than in production. Nevertheless, her argument that textual critique in isolation is not enough, and her recommendations for future film criticism, coincide with my comments here about literary criticism. The point is that the critical analysis of representation has to be integrated with a more sociological account of the conditions and institutions of the production and reception of those texts. Annette Kuhn has explored this possibility more systematically in her book *Women's Pictures*, in which she reviews work on the analysis of filmic texts as well as examining the film industry and the social relations of the making (and viewing) of films, both feminist and in the mainstream. She is quite clear that text and institution have to be seen together: 'Put simply, the logic of dominant cinematic institutions works in the final instance towards the production of dominant meanings.' And this, of course, has implications for feminist cinema too, for as she says 'as signifying practice, feminist countercinema must be conditioned by its institutional formation, just as dominant modes of cinematic representation . . . are formed in and by certain institutional apparatuses'.[44] Feminist literary criticism, in the same way, must begin to work towards a theoretical practice that exposes the ways in which dominant meanings are produced in dominant literary institutions.

I want to conclude with a comment about the relationship between criticism and politics. Toril Moi's own conclusion, based on her critical comparison of the two approaches, is that 'it is our task now to take feminist criticism one step further and transform it into the politically committed and the theoretically highly developed criticism it clearly has the potential to become'.[45] Feminist literary criticism, as part of the practice of the women's movement, is a political activity as much as an intellectual one. In some ways, the reminder of the political nature of criticism provides an instant confirmation of some of the points I have been making in a more theoretical way in this essay. For it is clearly absolutely crucial, for any intervention in criticism or in literary production itself, to start from a detailed knowledge of the institutions and social relations in which writing is produced; this strategic competence, essential for an effective politics, is the political counterpart of the intellectual adequacy required for feminist criticism and for a sociology of literature.[46]

NOTES

1 See, for example, Catherine Belsey, *Critical Practice* (London, Methuen, 1980); Terry Eagleton, *Literary Theory: An Introduction* (Oxford, Blackwell, 1983); Peter Widdowson (ed.), *Re-reading English* (London, Methuen, 1982); Janet Batsleer *et al.* (eds), *Rewriting English; Cultural Politics of Gender and Class* (London, Methuen, 1985).

2 Examples of such developments in art and music are A. L. Rees and F. Borzello (eds), *The New Art History* (London, Camden Press, 1986) and Richard E. Leppert and Susan McClary (eds), *Music and Society: The Politics of Composition, Performance and Reception* (Cambridge, Cambridge University Press, 1987).

3 This development in social science is discussed further in the

Introduction to Janet Wolff and John Seed (eds), *The Culture of Capital: Art, Power and the Nineteenth-Century Middle Class* (Manchester, Manchester University Press, 1988).

4   It makes sense to date this work in Britain from the foundation of the Centre for Contemporary Cultural Studies at the University of Birmingham in 1964; although most work in the United States dates from the mid-1970s, earlier studies in the sociology of art include Robert N. Wilson (ed.), *The Arts in Society* (Englewood Cliffs, Prentice-Hall, 1964), Harrison C. White and Cynthia A. White, *Canvases and Careers: Institutional Change in the French Painting World* (New York, John Wiley & Sons, 1965), and Vytautas Kavolis, *Artistic Expression: A Sociological Analysis* (Ithaca, Cornell University Press, 1968).

5   The Cambridge Women's Studies Group, *Women in Society: Interdisciplinary Essays* (London, Virago, 1981), p. 1.

6   For example, Jenni Calder, *Women and Marriage in Victorian Fiction* (London and New York, Oxford University Press, 1976); Nina Auerbach, *Woman and the Demon: The Life of a Victorian Myth* (Cambridge, Mass., Harvard University Press, 1982).

7   From Kate Millett, *Sexual Politics* (London, Hart-Davis, 1971) to more recent studies like Lisa Jardine's '*The Duchess of Malfi*: A Case Study in the Literary Representation of Women', in Susanne Kappeler and Norman Bryson (eds), *Teaching the Text* (London, Routledge & Kegan Paul, 1983).

8   For example, Jean E. Kennard, *Victims of Convention* (Hamden, Conn., Archon Books, 1978).

9   See, for example, Janice A. Radway, *Reading the Romance: Women, Patriarchy, and Popular Literature* (Chapel Hill, University of North Carolina Press, 1984); Rachel Blau DuPlessis, *Writing beyond the Ending: Narrative Strategies of Twentieth-Century Women Writers* (Bloomington, Indiana University Press, 1985); Marxist-Feminist Literature Collective, 'Women's Writing: *Jane Eyre, Shirley, Villette, Aurora Leigh*', in Francis Barker *et al.* (eds), *1848: The Sociology of Literature* (Colchester, University of Essex, 1978).

10   For example, Judith Fetterley, *The Resisting Reader: A Feminist Approach to American Fiction* (Bloomington, Indiana University Press, 1978); Jonathan Culler, 'Reading as a Woman', ch. 1, section 3, in *On Deconstruction. Theory and Criticism after Structuralism* (London, Routledge & Kegan Paul, 1983).

11   Auerbach, *Woman and the Demon*.

12   For example, Sandra M. Gilbert and Susan Gubar, *The Madwoman in the Attic: The Woman Writer and the Nineteenth-Century Literary Imagination* (New Haven, Conn., Yale University Press, 1979); Mary Jacobus, 'The Buried Letter: Feminism and Romanticism in *Villette*', in *Women Writing and Writing about Women* (London, Croom Helm, 1979).

13   See, for example, Women's Studies Group, Centre for Contemporary Cultural Studies, *Women Take Issue: Aspects of Women's Subordination* (London, 1978); Bridget Fowler, 'True to Me Always: An Analysis of Women's Magazine Fiction', and Rosalind Brunt, 'A Career in Love: the Romantic World of Barbara Cartland', both in Christopher Pawling (ed.), *Popular Fiction and Social Change* (London, Macmillan, 1984).

14   For example, by Elaine Showalter, in the introduction to Elaine Showalter (ed.), *The New Feminist Criticism: Essays on Women, Literature, and Theory* (London, Virago, 1986), pp. 8–9; and by Maggie Humm, in 'Feminist Literary Criticism in America and England', in Moira Monteith (ed.), *Women's Writing: A Challenge to Theory* (Brighton, Harvester, 1986).

15   For example, by Toril Moi, in *Sexual/Textual Politics* (London, Methuen, 1985).

16   Ibid. See also Elizabeth Abel (ed.), *Writing and Sexual Difference* (Brighton, Harvester, 1982); and Robert Young (ed.), *Sexual Difference* (special issue of *The Oxford Literary Review* (Southampton, 1986)).

17   Showalter presents these as consecutive developments (Introduction to *New Feminist Criticism*, p. 6). Examples of this type of work are Ellen Moers, *Literary Women: The Great Writers* (New York, Doubleday Anchor Press, 1977); Elaine Showalter, *A Literature of Their Own: British Women Novelists from Brontë to Lessing* (Princeton, NJ, Princeton University Press, 1977); Nina Baym, *Woman's Fiction: A Guide to Novels by and about Women in America, 1820–1870* (Ithaca, NY, Cornell University Press, 1978); Annette Kolodny, 'Some Notes on Defining a "Feminist Literary Criticism" ', *Critical Inquiry*, v. 2 (1975).

18   Eleanor Tufts, *Our Hidden Heritage: Five Centuries of Women Artists* (London, Paddington Press, 1974); Karen Petersen and J.J. Wilson, *Women Artists: Recognition and Reappraisal from the Early Middle Ages to the Twentieth Century* (New York, Harper & Row, 1976); Ann Sutherland Harris and Linda Nochlin, *Women Artists 1550–1950* (New York, Random House, 1976); Germaine Greer, *The Obstacle Race: The Fortunes of Women Painters and their Work* (London, Secker & Warburg, 1979).

19   Elaine Showalter, 'Feminist Criticism in the Wilderness', in Abel (ed.), *Writing and Sexual Difference*; also in 'Shooting the Rapids', in Young (ed.), *Sexual Difference*.

20   For example, Moers, *Literary Women*.

21   Examples of this work include Tony Davies, 'Education, ideology and literature', *Red Letters*, no. 7 (1978); Terry Eagleton, *The Function of Criticism: From* The Spectator *to Post-Structuralism* (London, Verso, 1984); Francis Mulhern, *The Moment of 'Scrutiny'* (London, New Left Books, 1979).

22   Terry Eagleton, *Criticism and Ideology: A Study in Marxist Literary Theory* (London, New Left Books, 1976), ch. 2.
23   Ibid., p. 48.
24   Terry Eagleton, *The Rape of Clarissa: Writing, Sexuality and Class Struggle in Samuel Richardson* (Oxford, Blackwell, 1982).
25   Raymond Williams, *Culture* (Glasgow, Fontana, 1986), pp. 30–1. (Italics in the original).
26   See, for example, 'Forms of English Fiction in 1848', in Barker *et al.* (eds.) *1848: The Sociology of Literature*, and reprinted in Raymond Williams, *Writing in Society* (London, Verso, 1983); also 'Notes on English Prose 1780–1950', in Williams, *Writing in Society*.
27   Examples are Peter H. Mann, *From Author to Reader: A Social Study of Books* (London, Routledge & Kegan Paul, 1982); J. A. Sutherland, *Fiction and the Fiction Industry* (London, Athlone Press, 1978); Lewis A. Coser, Charles Kadushin, and Walter W. Powell, *Books: The Culture and Commerce of Publishing* (New York, Basic Books, 1982).
28   Two collections of essays under this title are Richard A. Peterson (ed.), *The Production of Culture* (London, Sage, 1976) and Lewis A. Coser (ed.), *The Production of Culture*, *Social Research*, 45, no. 2 (Summer 1978). Other similar collections, originating in the annual Social Theory and the Arts Conferences (now known as Social Theory, Politics and the Arts), are Jack B. Kamerman and Rosanne Martorella (eds), *Performers and Performances: The Social Organization of Artistic Work* (New York, Praeger, 1982) and Judith H. Balfe and Margaret Jane Wyszomirski (eds.), *Art, Ideology and Politics* (New York, Praeger, 1985).
29   But on the impossibility of this separation of the aesthetic and the sociological, see Elizabeth Bird, 'Aesthetic Neutrality and the Sociology of Art', in Michèle Barrett *et al.* (eds), *Ideology and Cultural Production* (London, Croom Helm, 1979). See also Janet Wolff, *Aesthetics and the Sociology of Art* (London, Allen & Unwin, 1983).
30   On the need for a sociology of texts and institutions, see Janet Wolff, 'The Problem of Ideology in the Sociology of Art: A Case Study of Manchester in the Nineteenth Century', *Media, Culture and Society*, 4, 1 (January 1982).
31   This is attempted, for example, by Barbara Rosenblum, in *Photographers at Work: A Sociology of Photographic Styles* (New York, Holmes & Meier, 1978).
32   The same criticism can be applied to the sociology of the visual arts, which has also tended to investigate social structure and to ignore the visual text; see, for example, White and White, *Canvases and Careers*.
33   Gaye Tuchman and Nina Fortin, 'Edging Women out: Some Suggestions about the Structure of Opportunities and the Victorian

Novel', *Signs*, 6, no. 2 (1980). See also Lynne Spender, *Intruders on the Rights of Men* (London, Pandora Press, 1983); and Michele Caplette, 'Women in Book Publishing: A Qualified Success Story', in Coser, Kadushin, and Powell (eds), *Books: The Culture and Commerce of Publishing*, ch. 6.

34   Moi, *Sexual/Textual Politics*. See also her article, 'Sexual/Textual Politics', in Francis Barker (ed.), *The Politics of Theory* (Colchester, University of Essex, 1983).

35   For example, some recent readers and collections of essays in feminist literary criticism include work from both perspectives. See Showalter (ed.), *New Feminist Criticism*; Mary Eagleton (ed.), *Feminist Literary Theory: A Reader* (Oxford, Blackwell, 1986); Gayle Greene and Coppélia Kahn (eds), *Making a Difference: Feminist Literary Criticism* (London, Methuen, 1985).

36   Moi, 'Sexual/textual politics', p. 1.

37   See Rozsika Parker and Griselda Pollock, *Old Mistresses: Women, Art and Ideology* (London, Routledge & Kegan Paul 1981), ch. 4; Helene E. Roberts, 'Marriage, Redundancy or Sin: The Painter's View of Women in the First Twenty-Five Years of Victoria's Reign', in Martha Vicinus (ed.), *Suffer and Be Still: Women in the Victorian Age* (Bloomington, Indiana University Press, 1972); Lynda Nead, 'Woman as Temptress: The Siren and the Mermaid in Victorian Painting', *Leeds Arts Calendar*, 91 (1982).

38   Parker and Pollock, *Old Mistresses*; Griselda Pollock, 'Feminism, Femininity and the Hayward Annual Exhibition 1978', *Feminist Review*, 2 (1979).

39   'Sex, Text, Politics: An Interview with Victor Burgin', by Tony Godfrey, *Block*, 7 (1982), p. 2.

40   Ibid., p. 25. (Italics in the original.)

41   Griselda Pollock, 'Art, Artschool, Culture: Individualism after the Death of the Artist', *Block*, 11 (1985/6). See also her 'History and Position of the Contemporary Woman Artist', *Aspects*, 28 (Autumn 1984).

42   Deborah Cherry and Griselda Pollock, 'Woman as Sign in Pre-Raphaelite Literature: A Study of the Representation of Elizabeth Siddall', *Art History*, 7, 2 (June 1984).

43   Claire Johnston, 'The Subject of Feminist Film Theory/Practice', *Screen* 21, no. 2 (Summer 1980), p. 28.

44   Annette Kuhn, *Women's Pictures: Feminism and Cinema* (London, Routledge & Kegan Paul, 1982).

45   Moi, 'Sexual/Textual Politics', pp. 11–12.

46   Feminist literary criticism has, at least until very recently, been predominantly about the situation and representation of white women; it has also been dominated in its concerns by a heterosexual perspective. Black women and lesbians are developing their own critical approaches, in relation both to patriarchal culture and to white, heterosexist, feminist criticism. See the articles by Bonnie

Zimmerman and Susan Willis in Greene and Kahn (eds), *Making a Difference*;   by Barbara Smith and Deborah F. McDowell in Showalter (ed.), *New Feminist Criticism* (in which Zimmerman's essay is also included); by Gayatri Chakravorty Spivak in Young (ed.), *Sexual Difference*; and extracts from essays by Adrienne Rich, Alice Walker, Gayatri Chakravorty Spivak, Bonnie Zimmerman, Barbara Smith, Black Woman Talk Collective, and Deborah E. McDowell, in Eagleton (ed.), *Feminist Literary Theory*. The arguments I have been developing in this essay with regard to feminist criticism apply equally to the criticism and politics of black women and lesbian women, whose effective intervention and critique depends on the strategic grasp of social and cultural relations at least as much as on adequate textual readings.

8

Reinstating Corporeality:
Feminism and Body Politics

Is the body a site of cultural and political protest? And can women's bodies be the site of feminist cultural politics? These are currently contested issues.

> I do not see how . . . there is any possibility of using the image of a naked woman . . . other than in an absolutely sexist and politically repressive patriarchal way in this conjuncture.[1]

> To use the body of the woman, her image or person is not impossible but problematic for feminism.[2]

Crucial to the debate about the political potential of the body is the more fundamental question of whether there *is* any body outside discourse – another matter of dispute.

> Experience of the body even at the simplest level is mediated by a presentation of the body, the body-image.[3]

> The positing of a body *is* a condition of discursive practices.[4]

In this essay I will argue for a cultural politics of the body, based on a recognition of the social and discursive construction of the body, while emphasizing its lived experience and materiality.

The Dangers of Body Politics

On 17 July 1989, a group of women staged a protest against the sole use by men of a bathing area at Sandycove, Dublin. The men often swam naked in this area, an artificial harbour on the seafront called Forty Foot pool. The women's protest was to invade the area and to remove their own swimming suits. The reporting of this event makes clear the ambiguities and ultimate failure of such body politics. The *Guardian* carried a short note, as a caption to a photograph (Plate 9). The photo depicts one of the women, facing the camera and walking out of the water, wearing only a small pair of briefs. Behind her men and boys in small boats stare. She walks past a line of young boys, who gawp at her body and laugh at her. It is not an attractive scene. Without having been at the event, one can only assume that female nudity achieved nothing more than male lechery. Moreover, the photograph in the press the next morning renders the liberal (and generally pro-feminist) paper the *Guardian* little different from the tabloids, with their Page Three topless pinups. The political gesture is neutralized and doubly cancelled – first by the look of those at the scene, and second by its representation in the press for the reader's gaze. The lesson (or one of them) is that there are problems with using the female body for feminist ends. Its pre-existing meanings, as sex object, as object of the male gaze, can always prevail and reappropriate the body, despite the intentions of the woman herself.

This can also occur with less naïve interventions, which incorporate a critical understanding of the meanings and uses of the female body in our culture. The movie *Not a Love Story* is a documentary about the pornography industry, made by women and presenting a clearly feminist and critical view of pornography. When it arrived in Leeds in the early 1980s, however, it was for some reason shown in one of the rather sleazy city-centre cinemas. Its audience consisted of a few groups of women (the film had not had much advance publicity, and this, together with the rather peculiar venue, meant that large numbers of local feminists did not turn up), and a considerable contingent from the raincoat brigade. Individual men were scattered throughout the cinema. And the point is that they would not have been disappointed, for, as sympathetic critics have pointed out, in order to discuss the pornography industry, the movie spent a good deal of time showing pornographic images and sequences.[5] Again, this raises the question of whether, or how, women can engage in a critical politics of the body, in a culture which so comprehensively codes and defines women's bodies as subordinate and passive, and as objects of the male gaze. Peter Gidal's pessimism, in the first quotation with which I began this essay, is a well-founded one.

Yet I want to argue that a feminist cultural politics of the body *is* a possibility. As Mary Kelly says, this may be problematic, but it is not impossible. There is every reason, too, to propose the body as a privileged site of political intervention, precisely because it is the site of repression and possession. The body has been systematically repressed and marginalized in Western culture, with specific practices, ideologies, and discourses controlling and defining the female body. What is repressed, though, may threaten to erupt and challenge the established order. It is on such grounds that some have argued for a body politics, and some feminists have urged a cultural and political intervention which is grounded in, and which employs, the body. I shall review these arguments, in order to draw some conclusions about the prospects for a feminist body politics in contemporary culture.

Repression and Marginalization of the Body in Western Culture

As Mary Douglas has shown, the body operates as a symbol of society across cultures, and the rituals, rules, and boundaries concerning bodily behaviour can be understood as the functioning of social rules and hierarchies.[6] In some cultures, bodily refuse (excreta, blood, tears, hair, nail clippings) has magical, and dangerous, qualities. In its marginality, in the way in which it traverses the boundaries of the body, it comes to represent particular threats and powers, which ultimately symbolize social boundaries, transgressions, and threats. What counts as pollution varies from society to society, but in all cases, according to Douglas, it is a 'symbolic system, based on the image of the body, whose primary concern is the ordering of a social hierarchy'.[7]

There is a wonderful scene in Bunuel's film *The Phantom of Liberty* in which a bourgeois couple arrives for a dinner party. With the usual social pleasantries and exchanges, they are led by the hosts to join the others. The guests are all seated round a large dining table, but the table is not laid for a meal. Instead, it is covered by magazines. The guests leaf through these casually, while exchanging remarks. Each guest is sitting on a toilet. After a while, one of the guests discreetly excuses himself, stands up, adjusts his dress, flushes the toilet, and leaves the room. He goes to a small closet, locks the door behind him, and sits down. Then he pulls down a tray of food from the wall, and eats this in privacy, before going back to join the others.

This scene, of course, illustrates graphically the arbitrary nature of our social customs – specifically those that deal with appropriate and acceptable bodily behaviour. We might rush to argue that there are *objective* reasons, of health, hygiene, cleanliness, for eating in public and defecating in private. But Mary Douglas's work clearly shows that these are only rationalizations. In this, 'civilized' customs are no different from 'primitive' customs. The discourse is one of cleanliness and hygiene, but in all cases the hidden meanings are those of social order and social hierarchy. This crucial anthropological perspective helps us to make sense of the particular, and peculiar, development of regimes of the body in Western culture.

Norbert Elias's pioneering study, *The Civilizing Process*, analyses the development and sophistication of manners in relation to social transformations in Europe in the sixteenth century and since. In particular he perceives the growth of notions of *intimacy* as part of the rise and consolidation of an intellectual class, which was able to distance itself from other classes, including the ruling strata. Manners thus serve as differentiating characteristics. Erasmus's *De civilatate morum puerilium* of 1530 was a key text, a turning point in the literature of manners and civilized behaviour. Elias makes his point most clearly by straightforward quotation from earlier and later handbooks on manners. Examples from the Middle Ages include: 'A man who clears his throat when he eats and one who blows his nose in the tablecloth are both ill-bred, I assure you.' And 'If a man snorts like a seal when he eats, as some people do, and smacks his chops like a Bavarian yokel, he has given up all good breeding.'[28]

In Erasmus, we already have a much greater refinement of behaviour, though not yet one which we would recognize as 'civilized' by our own contemporary standards.

Your goblet and knife, duly cleansed, should be on the right, your bread on the left.
Some people put their hands in the dishes the moment they have sat down. Wolves do that . . .
To dip the fingers in the sauce is rustic. You should take what you want with your knife and fork. . . .

To lick greasy fingers or to wipe them on your coat is impolite. It is better to use the tablecloth or the serviette.[9]

And, with regard to behaviour in the bedroom, Erasmus recommends: 'If your share a bed with a comrade, lie quietly; do not toss with your body, for this can lay yourself bare or inconvenience your companion by pulling away the blankets. . . . If you share a bed with another man, keep still.'[10] By 1729, a couple of centuries later, the rules of the bedroom were stricter. 'You ought neither to undress nor go to bed in the presence of any other person. Above all, unless you are married, you should not go to bed in the presence of anyone of the other sex. . . . When you get up you should not leave the bed uncovered, nor put your nightcap on a chair or anywhere else where it can be seen.'[11]

In the civilizing process, the body is increasingly patrolled, the range of acceptable behaviour increasingly carefully and narrowly defined. Emerging from this process of gradual exclusion and privatization of areas of bodily functions is what Bakhtin called the 'classical body'. The classical body has no orifices and engages in no base bodily functions. It is like a classical statue. It is opposed to the 'grotesque body', which has orifices, genitals, protuberances.[12] Francis Barker's fascinating study of seventeenth-century Europe documents the developing idea of the separation of the body from the soul, showing in relation to selected key texts (a Marvell poem, a Rembrandt painting, Pepys's diary) how the body was increasingly redefined and privatized, its sexual and other needs and appetites denied.[13] Like Elias, Barker analyses these transformations of discourse in relation to changes in class structure, labour demands, and the reconstitution of subjectivity. The 'positive body', founded on the exclusion of desires and appetites, which now consitute the 'absent body', is the ideal and necessary subject and object of rational science and bourgeois society.

Barker's analysis is indebted in turn to the work of Michel Foucault, particularly on the history of madness and the birth of the prison. From Foucault's detailed examination of the institutions of confinement, we have come to understand the construction in bourgeois society of the docile body[14] and the new forms of discipline (factories, schools, prisons, asylums) in which the most comprehensive surveillance has come to be exercised. The body is increasingly brought into discourse, and supervised, observed, and controlled by a variety of disciplines. In this process, and with the disappearance of older forms of bodily control such as torture, public spectacle and so on, control operates through internalization, and becomes, to a large extent, *self*-surveillance. At the same time, large areas of bodily experience, such as sexuality and illness, are delimited and redefined. As is well known, however, Foucault argues *against* the thesis that the nineteenth century witnessed a severe repression of sexuality. Rather, sexuality came increasingly into discourse, with the proliferation of disciplines and practices which spoke of it: medicine, psychiatry, sexology, and so on.[15] These processes have continued into the late twentieth century, where new forms of discipline in consumer society operate through advertising, fashion, popular culture and the market.[16]

Finally, the recognition that the body has been systematically denied and marginalized in Western culture, and that this development is closely related to the needs and ideologies of bourgeois capitalism (its construction of a particular notion of subjectivity, its requirement for a reliable, docile, regular workforce, its dependence on the self-regulation of its subjects), is confirmed by social historians, who have documented the control and elimination of working-class sports and popular recreations during and after the Industrial Revolution.[17] Blood sports, such as bull-baiting and cock-fighting, were criminalized in England in the first half of the nineteenth century (though upper-class pursuits like the hunt were not). Fairs were controlled, and football transformed from a game of the streets to an organized spectator sport by the end of the century. Licensing laws were intended to contain drinking habits. Behind these measures lay a mixture of concern to retain a reliable working population, fears about the political dangers of working-class gatherings, and ideological concerns linked to the class and domestic morality of the bourgeoisie.

If the body has thus been repressed since the seventeenth century, does it follow that the irruption of the 'grotesque' body, the explosion into visibility of its suppressed features (sex, laughter, excretion, and so on) constitutes a political revolution as well as a moral transgression? Stallybrass and White are rightly cautious about any blanket endorsement of bodily transgression as inherently radical.

> It would be wrong to associate the exhilarating sense of freedom which transgression affords with any necessary or automatic political progressiveness. . . . Often it is a powerful ritual or symbolic practice

whereby the dominant squanders its symbolic capital so as to get in touch with the fields of desire which it denied itself as the price paid for its political power. Not a repressive desublimation (for just as transgression is not intrinsically progressive, nor is it intrinsically conservative), it is a counter-sublimation, a delirious expenditure of the symbolic capital accrued (through the regulation of the body and the decathexis of habitus) in the successful struggle of bourgeois hegemony.[18]

Indeed, the transgressions of the carnivalesque and of the grotesque body can in many cases, as they also point out, operate in reactionary ways, particularly with regard to gender. This is something I shall return to.

The Female Body in Western Culture

Despite Foucault's radical argument that the nineteenth century saw an incitement to sex, not a repression of it, there is no question about the oppression of women through the discourses of the body. One collection of essays, largely inspired by Foucault's work, demonstrates the many ways in which contemporary discourses and practices rendered women inferior, put control of women's bodies into men's hands, and produced new sciences which redefined women and femininity centrally in terms of reproductive function, denying female sexuality while perceiving women as somehow closer to Nature than men.[19] This equation of woman with the body, for the most part a product of eighteenth- and nineteenth-century debates and ideologies,[20] has a pre-history in classical thought. Elizabeth Spelman has shown that Plato, despite an apparent commitment to the equality of the sexes (in *The Republic*, for example), believed that women exemplified the failure to value the soul above the body.[21] His somatophobia and his misogyny, she suggests, are closely linked. Here, then, we already have the notion that women are closer (too close) to the body compared with men. When we recognize the great value put on the soul or the mind as against the body (which is a central aspect of the process discussed by Barker, in which the 'positive body' of rational science excludes and obscures the 'absent body' of desires and appetites), the significance of the identification of women with the body is clear.

It is through the body, too, that women in our culture learn their own particular form of self-surveillance. Sandra Bartky identifies the 'panoptical male connoisseur' in women's consciousness.[22] The discursive practices which produce 'femininity' are in the culture and within women. Thus they diet, dress for certain effect, monitor their movement and gestures. Unlike Bartky, I do not conclude that radical social change will come about as a result of a refusal of particular definitions and demands of 'femininity' and the substitution of an 'as yet unimagined transformation of the female body',[23] for this addresses only the *effects* of gender inequalities. It is likely that any *new* definitions of 'femininity' would equally provide the basis for control and self-surveillance. But the perception is accurate, that it is through the body that women collude in their own oppression, and the specifically feminist slant on Foucault's analysis of the effects of discourse is an invaluable one.

Women learn as girls to monitor their appearance, and to conform to what is presented in the culture as some ideal of femininity. A group of German women explored in discussion the ways in which this policing (and self-policing) works, and how early it begins.

> Every Thursday afternoon, the park was open to me for free; I had a special pass to let me in for my gym lesson. My mother had put my name down for the class so I could do something about my weak stomach muscles. She said the only way I could get rid of my tummy at my age was by strengthening the muscles with exercise. In a few years' time, when I was grown up, I'd then be able to deal with it by pulling it in.[24]

Advertising and the fashion industry show us the perfect body for women, though, as Rosalind Coward has said, this ideal shifts slightly from one season to the next.[25]

> If you just *love* being a girl (and really look like one), this is *your* time! After decades of 'You can never be too rich or too thin', the all-girl girl has reemerged to be celebrated and adored. Curves à la Monroe (if she'd worked out a bit more!) are what's red-hot right now. So if you've been disguising all those luscious lines under industrial-strength bras and baggy sweaters, stop! Here are a few suggestions for really showing *off* this shapely, gorgeous girl.[26]

(It is noticeable, however, that the all-girl girl still has a small waist and perfectly flat stomach. There are apparently limits to the revolution in body ideal.)

Cultural theory, particularly in the visual arts and film studies, has explored for a decade and a half the representation of women's bodies in patriarchal culture, informed first by John Berger's early perception that paintings of the nude in Western art imply a male spectator and are constructed for the male gaze, and then by Laura Mulvey's influential article of 1975, which analyzed the operation of the male gaze and the representation of the female body in film in terms of psychoanalytic theory.[27] The issue of women's viewing positions and possible identifications has been one much discussed (and disputed) in recent years, though this is not something I shall consider here. The devastating implication of this work in general appears to be that women's bodies (particularly the nude, though not just that) *cannot* be portrayed other than through the regimes of representation which produce them as objects for the male gaze, and as the projection of male desires. The failure of the Dublin intervention should have been predicted, in the light of this. We have to ask what this means for feminist art practice (can women paint women's bodies? are there ways of subverting or circumventing the dominant modes of representation?) and for body politics (*can* the body, after all, be a site of cultural critique?).

Transgression and the Female Body

What happens when the female body is affirmed and displayed, in defiance of the dominant ideals of the 'perfect body', acknowledging the reality of actual women, the diversities of shape and size, the functions of corporeal existence (eating, excreting, menstruation, sex, pregnancy, aging, illness)? The 'grotesque body', at least, should be immune from incorporation into the objectifying gaze. (The question of hard-core pornography, which depends on a particular deviation from the classical to the grotesque body, is an interesting one, requiring a more complex analysis of such imagery in relation to sexuality and representation in patriarchal society. It is something I shall have to leave to one side, however.)

Mary Russo considers the female grotesques of carnival. The examples she discusses are unruly women (including men cross-dressing as women, in this role) in popular uprisings in seventeenth-century England, terracotta figurines of 'senile, pregnant hags' (discussed by Bakhtin) and Charcot's famous photographs of women hysterics.[28] She concludes that these figures are deeply ambivalent. As she says, 'women and their bodies, certain bodies, in certain public framings, in certain public spaces, are always already transgressive – dangerous and in danger'.[29] These cases and images of women 'in excess' of the idealized feminine may operate as threat (as well as example to other women). However, there are always reactionary connotations. The unruly woman is pilloried as a scold, henpecking her husband. Cross-dressing men are as likely to be portraying women with contempt as with respect. The image of the pregnant hag is 'loaded with all of the connotations of fear and loathing associated with the biological processes of reproduction and of aging'.[30] Female hysterics have a history of being locked up and contained. And at fairs and carnival festivities women were frequently abused and raped.

In any case, the excesses and reversals of the carnivalesque often operate to reaffirm the status quo, providing licensed but limited occasions for transgressions which are guaranteed to be neutralized. Whether or not there is any leakage into the culture in general from such occasions is an important question, though it is not one to which we can assume a positive answer. What I think we *can* safely affirm is the importance of the appearance itself of such transgressive images, practices, and ideas, for they render visible the suppressed. As Mary Russo says, how the category of the grotesque 'might be used affirmatively to destabilize the idealizations of female beauty or to realign the mechanisms of desire' is the subject of another study.[31] Like her, at this stage I simply note the potential value of the existence of spaces for the female grotesque body for the daunting project of the subversion of its dominant construction and portrayal.

Related to the notion of the female grotesque is Julia Kristeva's concept of the 'monstrous-feminine.' In her psychoanalytic account, the maternal body is the object of horror, a feeling based in the fear of reincorporation into the mother, as well as in the fear of the mother's generative power. In becoming a subject, with defined boundaries, the child is separating from the body of the mother. As a result the maternal body becomes 'abject' – an object of horror and threat.[32] Although Kristeva does not discuss this as a specifically gendered process, other recent work in psychoanalytic theory suggests that it is particularly the *male* child who confronts the trauma of separation, and who retains into adulthood the fear of reincorporation (and, hence, loss of masculinity and self).[33] This psychic process, undergone in a culture where it is women who do the mothering, explains the barely concealed level of violent fantasy men often manifest against women, the well-known construction of the virgin/whore dichotomy which counterposes the 'pure' woman (the classical body?) to the slut (the grotesque?). As Barbara Ehrenreich has put it, in a foreword to Klaus Theweleit's shocking study of male fantasies about women:

> It seems to me that as long as women care what we are in this world – at best, 'social inferiors', and at worst, a form of filth – then the male ego will be formed by, and bounded by, hideous dread. For that which they loved first – woman and mother – is that which they must learn to despise in others and suppress within themselves. Under these conditions, which are all we know, so far, as the human condition, men will continue to see the world as divided into 'them' and 'us', male and female, hard and soft, solid and liquid – and they will, in every way possible, fight and flee the threat of submersion. They will build dykes against the 'streaming' of their own desire. . . . They will confuse, in some mad revery, love and death, sex and murder.[34]

Discussions about the female body in terms of abjection, or the monstrous-feminine, tend to operate on different levels, and to refer to rather different aspects of psychic processes. Sometimes they concern the Oedipal drama and the fear of castration. Sometimes they are based in a theory of fetishism (the phallic woman). At other times they rely on a psychoanalytic account that stresses the pre-Oedipal moment, and deal with the need for separation and consequent fear of re-engulfment which I have been discussing. A more Lacanian version is based on the threat to the man's place in the Symbolic, which produces a resistance to the pre-Symbolic (and the mother). Yet another version rests on the fear of maternal authority, or of the power of the 'archaic' mother. All these accounts can be found in current film studies and cultural theory, and it is not my intention to assess or compare them. The general question raised by the notion of the 'monstrous-feminine', whatever its presumed origins, is whether it renders the (abject) body a potential site of transgression and feminist intervention. And I think our answer must be in terms of the same guarded optimism with which I considered the female grotesque: namely that the operative word is 'potential', for the dominant culture of patriarchy has already defined and situated the body, and the prospects for reappropriation are, to say the least, fraught with hazards and contradictions.

A third area of feminist body politics is what has been called '*l'écriture féminine*'. A concept originating in what is generally referred to as French feminism, this notion has a number of slightly different manifestations, of which I shall briefly discuss two.[35] In *La Révolution de langage poétique*, Julia Kristeva contrasts the realm and language of the Symbolic (the law of the Father, identified with and coincident with the coming into language of the child) with what she calls the 'semiotic'. The semiotic is the pre-linguistic, the bodily drives, rhythms, and 'pulsions' experienced by the child in the infantile fusion with the mother. These pleasures and feelings are repressed on entry into the Symbolic, but, according to Kristeva, since they remain in the unconscious, they may emerge at a later stage. In the writing of Lautréamont and Mallarmé, as well as Joyce and Artaud, the experience of the semiotic is articulated. (The term '*l'écriture féminine*' is not Kristeva's, and of course her examples of this kind of writing here are all of men. However, the 'feminine' nature of the writing consists of its supposed origins in the pre-Symbolic, pre-patriarchal moment of the child–mother relationship.)

Kristeva is well aware that it makes no sense to propose the semiotic as somehow outside of language. In the first place, she is talking about writing, which is necessarily linguistic. And in the second place, the writers she discusses are, like everyone else, in the Symbolic – an essential condition of human development. 'The semiotic that "precedes" symbolization is only a *theoretical supposition* justified by the need for description. It exists in practice only within the symbolic and requires the symbolic break to obtain the complex articulation we associate with it in musical and poetic practices.'[36]

Nevertheless, her argument is that there is possible a particular kind of writing that originates in the pre-linguistic, bodily experiences of infancy that have persisted in the unconscious into adulthood. Inasmuch as such writing subverts the Symbolic, it can therefore be seen (and has been so, by some feminists) as 'feminine' – both in the sense that its origins are in the pre-Oedipal child–mother relationship, and in the sense that it escapes the rule of the Father and the dominance of patriarchal language and thought .

Luce Irigaray and Hélène Cixous have proposed a more direct relationship between women, writing, and the body, one in which men could not be the agents of 'feminine writing'. Both begin from the specificity of woman's body – for Irigaray, a plural, multiple, diffuse sexuality, for Cixous, similarly multiple libidinal impulses (oral, anal, vocal, the pleasures of pregnancy). Woman, says Cixous, must 'write from the body': 'Her libido is cosmic, just as her unconscious is worldwide. Her writing can only keep going, without ever inscribing or discerning contours. . . . She alone dares and wishes to know from within, where she, the outcast, has never ceased to hear the resonance of fore-language.'[37] *L'écriture féminine* is writing grounded in women's experience of the body and sexuality, an experience which is not mediated by men and by patriarchy. This has been found to be an exceptionally liberating and suggestive notion by many feminists, who perceive in it the prospect of a cultural practice which is not compromised and contained by patriarchal discourses. The painter, Nancy Spero, has referred to her work as *la peinture féminine*, on the model of 'feminine writing', which, as Lisa Tickner says, commenting on Spero's work, is 'a form of writing marked by the pulsions of a female sexual body . . . and effecting various kinds of displacement on the western phallogocentric tradition of writing and the subject'.[38] In the next section of this essay, I will look at some of the problems involved in the notion of 'writing from the body' as feminist practice.

Discourse and the Body

One objection to the kind of body politics just discussed is that identifying women with their bodies is perilously close to those reactionary arguments in sociobiology and other disciplines, as well as in conservative common sense, which justify women's oppression in terms of their biology – size, hormones, lack of strength, child-bearing functions, lactation, monthly cycles, and so on. So, for example, Judy Chicago's famous art work, *The Dinner Party*, which celebrates the hidden history of women, and, amongst other things, employs vaginal imagery to represent selected women from the past, has been criticized by other feminists for this equation of women with their biology (and specifically their genitals).[39] This is a complex issue, for there is also every reason to want to affirm that which is denied or denigrated, and to assert the specificity and experience of the female body.

Related to this is the objection that *what* the female body is varies by culture, by century, and by social group. It is a social, historical, and ideological construct. (As I argued earlier, it is clear that, for example, medical science has 'made' the female body into a new entity in the modern age.) Biology is always overlaid and mediated by culture, and the ways in which women experience their own bodies is largely a product of social and political processes. The charge of 'essentialism' is a serious one – that is, the criticism that concepts like *l'écriture féminine* often depend on an assumed basic, unchanging identity of 'woman' and women's bodies, which ignores the realities of historical change, social production, and ideological construction. Elizabeth Gross has produced a carefully judged assessment of this debate, which I think is worth adopting, and which leaves us with the insights of Kristeva and Irigaray without the problems of an unacceptable essentialism: 'Both these feminists have shown that *some* concept of the body is essential to understanding social production, oppression and resistance; and that the body need not, indeed must not be considered merely a biological entity, but can be seen as a socially inscribed, historically marked, psychically and interpersonally significant product.'[40] The female body is seen as psychically and socially produced and inscribed. At the same time, it is experienced by women – primarily as lacking or incomplete. The feminist project of Irigaray, 'to speak about a positive model or series of representations of femininity by which the female body may be positively marked',[41] is endorsed by Gross.

The more radical version of this critique of essentialism argues that *there is no body outside discourse*. Parveen Adams's argument, indicated in the third quotation at the beginning of this essay, is the psychoanalytic one that we never have an unmediated experience of a pre-given body, but rather that perceptions of the body are 'represented from the start as agreeable or disagreeable'.[42] The experience of the body is always mediated by libidinal energy. To this we may add the parallel argument that the body is never experienced except as mediated through language and discourse. As I have already shown, the 'body' is a product of social histories, social relations, and discourses, all of which define it, identify its key features (ignoring others), prescribe and proscribe its behaviour. With regard to women's bodies, Denise Riley follows through this perception to conclude that whether and when bodies are *gendered* 'is a function of historical categorisations as well as of an individual daily phenomenology'.[43] The body is not always lived or treated as sexed. For, as she points out in relation to the politics of maternity:

If women did not have the capacity of childbearing they could not be arrayed by natalist or anti-natalist plans into populations to be cajoled or managed. But the point is that irrespective of natural capacities, only some prior lens which intends to focus on 'women's bodies' is going to set them in such a light. The body becomes visible *as* a body, and *as* a female body, only under some particular gaze – including that of politics.[44]

There can, therefore, be no 'direct' experience of the body, and we cannot talk about, or even conceive of, the body as some pre-given entity. This is as true for men as it is for women, but the particular implication here is that we need to be very careful in talking about a feminist body politics, whether one of *l'écriture féminine* or one of celebration of the female body. What constitutes the body, and what constitutes the female body and its experience, is already implicated in language and discourse. But this does not mean we must abandon the project. Recent developments in linguistics, psychoanalysis, and cultural theory have achieved the important task of challenging essentialism and naïve realism, and of deconstructing the category of 'woman', demonstrating its construction in psychic processes, social and historical relations, ideological struggles, and discursive formations. But there are pragmatic, political, and philosophical reasons for resisting a total agnosticism of the body. As Denise Riley puts it, 'it is compatible to suggest that "women" don't exist – while maintaining a politics of "as if they existed" – since the world behaves as if they unambiguously did'.[45]

In the first place, then, the instability of the category 'woman' and the specific objection to identifying women with the female body (itself seen to be ill-defined and not a constant), need not lead to the conclusion that the subject is irrevocably dispersed. There is some agreement among feminists that deconstruction, post-structuralism, and postmodernist theory are valuable allies in feminist analysis, critique, and political action, since they operate to destabilize patriarchal orthodoxies and also to oppose mistaken notions of uniform female identity.[46] At the same time, politically and experientially, it makes sense for women to mobilize around the social construct of 'woman' for, as Riley says, modern feminism 'is landed with the identity of women as an achieved fact of history and epistemology'.[47] To that extent, too, the female body, as discursively and socially constructed, and as currently experienced by women, may form the basis of a political and cultural critique – so long as it is one which eschews a naïve essentialism and incorporates the self-reflexivity of a recognition of the body as an effect of practices, ideologies, and discourses.

Finally, inconsistencies of the more radical anti-essentialist position have been pointed out. In the context of feminist film theory, Mary Ann Doane sees essentialism and anti-essentialism as opposite but equivalent mistakes.

> Both the proposal of a pure access to a natural female body and the rejection of attempts to conceptualize the female body based on their contamination by ideas of 'nature' are inhibiting and misleading. Both positions deny the necessity of posing a complex relation between the body and psychic-signifying processes, of using the body, in effect, as a 'prop'. For Kristeva is right – the positing of the body *is* a condition of discursive practices. It is crucial that feminism move beyond the opposition between essentialism and anti-essentialism.[48]

As she says, the question about the relation between the female body and language, raised by deconstructionists and discourse theorists, is a question about a relation between two terms.[49] In other words, the critique of essentialism does *not* amount to a proof that there *is* no body.

In the following section, I will draw some preliminary conclusions from this discussion about the prospects of a feminist cultural politics of the body, which need not be doomed to negation or reincorporation by the male gaze and by a patriarchal culture.

Gender, Dance, and Body Politics

Since the body is clearly marginalized in Western culture, it might appear that dance is an inherently subversive activity. Indeed, the marginality of dance itself as an art form in the West suggests that this is so – compared with orchestral music, opera, film, and literature, dance has had minority appeal. But we must beware of making the easy assumption that use of the body is itself transgressive, in a culture which allows only the 'classical body'. Here, from a key text on dance, is an accredited discussion of the ballet.

> The bearing of the classical dancer . . . is characterized by compactness. The thigh muscles are drawn up, the torso rests upon the legs like a bust

upon its base. This bust swivels and bends but, in most *adagio* movements at any rate, the shoulders remain parallel to the pelvis bone. Every
bend, every jump is accomplished with an effect of ease and of lightness
. . . In all such convolutions of the *adagio* the ballerina is showing the
many gradual planes of her body in terms of harmonious lines. While
her arms and one leg are extended, her partner turns her slowly round
upon the pivot of her straight point. She is shown to the world with
utmost love and grace. She will then integrate herself afresh, raise herself
on the points, her arms close together, the one slightly in front of the
other. It is the alighting of the insect, the shutting of the wings, the
straightening into the perpendicular of feelers and of legs. Soon she will
take flight and extend herself again. Meanwhile she shows us on the
points what we have not seen in the *arabesque* or *développé*, two
unbroken lines from toes to thighs.[50]

The classical ballet has colluded in the preservation of the
classical body, emphasizing in its commitment to line, weightless-
ness, lift, and extension an ethereal presence rather than a real
corporeality. In addition, the strict limits on body size and shape for
girls and women dancers reinforce a denial of the female body in
favour of an ideal of boyish petiteness. (It is no surprise that the
incidence of eating disorders among ballerinas and would-be
ballerinas is far higher than that among the general population.[51])
The roles created for women in the classical repertoire – fairies,
swans, innocent peasant girls – collude in a discourse which
constructs, in a medium which employs the body for its expression,
a strangely disembodied female.

Modern dance, from its beginnings early in the twentieth century,
has usually been seen as an important breakthrough for women. For
one thing, many of the major innovators and choreographers in
modern dance have been women, unlike the classical ballet which
has always been dominated by men. Isadora Duncan, Martha
Graham, Doris Humphreys, and Mary Wigman are among the key
figures here. The modern repertoire also consists of many pieces
which deal with strong women, and with myths and stories from
women's point of view. Most important, modern dance has totally
transformed the types of movement seen on the stage, abandoning
the purity of line and denial of weight of the classical ballet, and
introducing angularity, pelvic movement, emphasis on the body's
weight and its relationship to the ground. A notion of the 'natural
body' has been employed in this development, particularly by
Duncan and Graham and their followers. This particular combina-

tion, of a conception of the natural body, and a commitment to women's stories and lives, has led many practitioners and critics to conclude that modern dance *is* a medium for political as well as aesthetic transgression.

But, as the critique of essentialism has shown, we must be wary of a cultural politics which is based on any notion of women's natural body, or women's universal essence – the kind of conception, for example, which lies behind many of Martha Graham's representations of Greek myths. What this means is that dance can only be subversive when it questions and exposes the construction of the body in culture. In doing so, it necessarily draws attention to itself *as* dance – a version of the Brechtian device of laying bare the medium. Postmodern dance has begun to achieve this, and thus to use the body for the first time in a truly political way. This development is discussed by Elizabeth Dempster, who stresses that the key focus of postmodern dance (going back to Merce Cunningham in the 1940s, but for the most part emerging in the 1960s and 1970s) has been the body itself.[52] It is not uncommon for a postmodern choreographer to use untrained bodies in a work, alongside trained dancers. (Michael Clark's work is a British example of this practice.) Dance itself is thus deconstructed, and the operations and actions of the body made clear. The body itself may be the theme of the dance, and a good deal of postmodern dance is concerned with gender and sexual politics (Yvonne Rainer in the United States, DV8 in Britain). The repertoire, the style, the ideologies, and the illusion of transparency of the medium of both classical and modern dance have been overturned by postmodern dance. In such a practice, the body can indeed provide a site for a radical cultural politics.

The implications for a feminist politics of the body are clear, not just for dance, which is necessarily founded on the body as its medium of expression, but also for visual representation, performance art, and other arts disciplines. A straightforward celebratory art of the female body may have the welcome effect of producing positive images for women, in defiance of the dominant constructions of femininity in our culture. At the same time, it runs two kinds of risk: first, that these images can be re-appropriated by the dominant culture, and read against the grain of their intended meaning (as in the Dublin demonstration); and second that they may collude with a kind of sexist thinking which identifies woman with the body, and assumes an unchanging, pre-given essence of the female. Any body politics, therefore, must speak *about* the body, stressing its materiality and its social and discursive construction, at the same time as disrupting and subverting existing regimes of representation. Feminist artists and critics have suggested strategies for this kind of intervention, including ironic quotation of works by men, juxtapositions of text and image which challenge representation, addressing the construction of femininity in the work itself, incorporating the self-reflexive commentary on the mode of representation employed, and what Mary Kelly has called the 'depropriation' of the image.[53]

Body politics need not depend on an uncritical, ahistorical notion of the (female) body. Beginning from the lived experience of women in their currently constituted bodily identities – identities which are *real* at the same time as being socially inscribed and discursively produced – feminist artists and cultural workers can engage in the challenging and exhilarating task of simultaneously affirming those identities, questioning their origins and ideological functions, and working towards a non-patriarchal expression of gender and the body.

NOTES

1   Peter Gidal, quoted by Mary Ann Doane, 'Woman's Stake: Filming the Female Body', in Constance Penley (ed.), *Feminism and Film Theory* (Routledge, New York and London, BFI Publishing, 1988), p. 217.
2   Mary Kelly, quoted by Rosemary Betterton, 'New Images for Old: The Iconography of the Body', in *Looking On: Images of Femininity in the Visual Arts and Media* (London and New York, Pandora, 1987), p. 206.
3   Parveen Adams, 'Versions of the Body', *m/f*, 11/12 (1986), p. 29.
4   Mary Ann Doane, 'Woman's Stake', p. 226.
5   See, for example, Susan Barrowclough, 'Not a Love Story', *Screen*, 23, 5 (1982).
6   Mary Douglas, *Purity and Danger: An Analysis of the Concepts of Pollution and Taboo* (1966; London and Boston, Routledge & Kegan Paul, 1984).
7   Ibid., p. 125.
8   Norbert Elias, *The Civilizing Process*, vol. 1: *The History of Manners* (Oxford, Blackwell, 1978), p. 64.
9   Ibid., pp. 89–90.
10   Ibid., pp. 161, 162.

11   Ibid., p. 162.
12   See Peter Stallybrass and Allon White, *The Politics and Poetics of Transgression* (London, Methuen, 1986), for an analysis of body imagery and social change in Europe from the seventeenth century, based on Bakhtin's division.
13   Francis Barker, *The Tremulous Private Body: Essays on Subjection* (London and New York, Methuen, 1984).
14   Michel Foucault, *Discipline and Punish: The Birth of the Prison* (Harmondsworth and New York, Penguin, 1979) pp. 135–69.
15   Michel Foucault, *The History of Sexuality*, vol. 1 *An Introduction* (London, Allen Lane, 1979).
16   See Mike Featherstone, 'The Body in Consumer Culture', *Theory, Culture and Society*, 1, 2 (September 1982).
17   See, for example, Robert Malcolmson, 'Popular Recreations under Attack', in Bernard Waites *et al.* (eds), *Popular Culture: Past and Present*. (London, Croom Helm, 1982).
18   Stallybrass and White, *Politics and Poetics of Transgression*, p. 201.
19   Catherine Gallagher and Thomas Laqueur (eds), *The Making of the Modern Body: Sexuality and Society in the Nineteenth Century* (Berkeley, Los Angeles and London, University of California Press, 1987).
20   See L.J. Jordanova, 'Natural Facts: A Historical Perspective on Science and Sexuality', in Carol MacCormack and Marilyn Strathern (eds), *Nature, Culture and Gender* Cambridge and New York, Cambridge University Press, 1980).
21   Elizabeth V. Spelman, 'Woman as Body: Ancient and Contemporary Views', *Feminist Studies*, 8, 1 (Spring 1982).
22   Sandra Lee Bartky, 'Foucault, Femininity, and the Modernization of Patriarchal Power', in Irene Diamond and Lee Quinby (eds), *Feminism and Foucault: Reflections on Resistance* (Boston, Northeastern University Press, 1988), p. 72.
23   Ibid., p. 79.
24   From Frigga Haug (ed.), *Female Sexualization: A Collective Work of Memory* (London, Verso, 1987), p. 126.
25   Rosalind Coward, *Female Desire* (London, Paladin, 1984) p. 39.
26   *Cosmopolitan* (US) (August 1989), p. 186.
27   John Berger, *Ways of Seeing* (Harmondsworth, Penguin, 1972); Laura Mulvey, 'Visual Pleasure and Narrative Cinema', *Screen*, 16, 3 (1975).
28   Mary Russo, 'Female Grotesques: Carnival and Theory', in Teresa de Lauretis (ed.) *Feminist Studies/Critical Studies* (London, Macmillan, 1986).
29   Ibid., p. 217.
30   Ibid., p. 219.
31   Ibid., p. 221.
32   Julia Kristeva, *Powers of Horror: An Essay on Abjection* (New York, Columbia University Press, 1982). Barbara Creed has used

this analysis in a most interesting way in the discussion of the basis of appeal of horror movies. (Barbara Creed, 'Horror and the Monstrous-Feminine: An Imaginary Abjection', *Screen*, 27, 1 (1986).)

33 See, for example, Evelyn Fox Keller, 'Gender and Science', in Sandra Harding and Merrill B. Hintikka (eds), *Discovering Reality: Feminist Perspectives on Epistemology, Metaphysics, Methodology, and Philosophy of Science* (Dordrecht, D. Reidel, 1983).

34 Barbara Ehrenreich, 'Foreword' to Klaus Theweleit, *Male Fantasies*, vol. 1: *Women, Floods, Bodies, History* (Minneapolis, University of Minnesota Press, 1987), p. xvi.

35 For a helpful discussion and critique of this term and its uses, see Ann Rosalind Jones, 'Writing the Body: Toward an Understanding of *l'écriture féminine*', in Elaine Showalter (ed.), *The New Feminist Criticism: Essays on Women, Literature, and Theory* (London, Virago, 1986).

36 Julia Kristeva, *Revolution in Poetic Language* (New York, Columbia University Press, 1984), p. 68.

37 Hélène Cixous, 'The Laugh of the Medusa', *Signs*, 1, 4 (Summer, 1976), p. 889. See also Luce Irigaray, *This Sex Which Is Not One* (Ithaca, NY, Cornell University Press, 1985).

38 Lisa Tickner, 'Nancy Spero: Images of Women and *la peinture féminine*', in *Nancy Spero* (London, Institute of Contemporary Arts, 1987), pp. 5, 7–8.

39 See, for example, Michèle Barrett, 'Feminism and the Definition of Cultural Politics', in C. Brunt and C. Rowan (eds), *Feminism, Culture and Politics* (London, Lawrence and Wishart, 1983).

40 Elizabeth Gross, 'Philosophy, Subjectivity and the Body: Kristeva and Irigaray', in Carole Pateman and Elizabeth Gross (eds), *Feminist Challenges: Social and Political Theory* (Boston, Northeastern University Press, 1986), p. 140.

41 Ibid., p. 142.

42 Adams, 'Versions of the Body', p. 29.

43 Denise Riley, *'Am I That Name?' Feminism and the Category of 'Women' in History* (Minneapolis, University of Minnesota Press, 1988), p. 105.

44 Ibid., p. 106.

45 Ibid., p. 112.

46 See, for example, Jane Flax, 'Postmodernism and Gender Relations in Feminist Theory', in *Signs*, 12, 4 (Summer 1987). Also *Feminist Studies*, 14, 1 (Spring 1988): special issue on deconstruction.

47 Riley, *'Am I That Name?'*, p. 111.

48 'Woman's Stake', pp. 225–6.

49 Ibid., p. 223.

50 Adrian Stokes, 'The Classical Ballet', extract from *Tonight the Ballet*, in Roger Copeland and Marshall Cohen (eds), *What is Dance? Readings in Theory and Criticism* (Oxford and New York, Oxford

University Press, 1983), pp. 244–5.

51   A personal account is the dancer Gelsey Kirkland's autobiography, *Dancing on my Grave* (London, Penguin, 1986).

52   Elizabeth Dempster, 'Women Writing the Body: Let's Watch a Little How She Dances', in Susan Sheridan (ed.), *Grafts: Feminist Cultural Criticism*, (London and New York, Verso, 1988).

53   Mary Kelly, 'Beyond the Purloined Image', *Block*, no. 9, (1983). See also Judith Barry and Sandy Flitterman, 'Textual Strategies: The Politics of Art-Making', *Screen*, 21, 2 (Summer 1980); and Lisa Tickner, 'The Body Politic: Female Sexuality and Women Artists since 1970', *Art History*, 1, 2 (June 1978) (repr. in Rosemary Betterton (ed.), *Looking on: Images of Femininity in the Visual Arts and Media* (London and New York, Pandora, 1987).)

Index